HOW TO DRAW
MANGA
Computones
Vol. 4

D1310127

CD-ROM Serial No.
CTWM30-300444079

HOW TO DRAW MANGA:
Computones Vol. 4
Portraying Couples
by Kuroyurihime

Copyright © 2006 Kuroyurihime
Copyright © 2006 Graphic-sha Publishing Co., Ltd.

This book was first designed and published in 2006 by Graphic-sha Publishing Co., Ltd.
Sansou Kudan Bldg., 4th Floor, 1-14-17 Kudan-kita, Chiyoda-ku, Tokyo 102-0073, Japan.

Original cover design and text page layout: Shinichi Ishioka
English translation management: Língua fránca, Inc. (an3y-skmt@asahi-net.or.jp)
Planning editor: Masahiko Satake (Graphic-sha Publishing Co., Ltd.)
Publishing coordinator: Yoko Ueno (Graphic-sha Publishing Co., Ltd.)
Project management: Kumiko Sakamoto (Graphic-sha Publishing Co., Ltd.)

First printing: May 2006

Cover:	Yayoi Koizumi
	Hisako Hiyama
Assistance:	Siawase Ninaru
	RYUJI.K
	Shiro Nakamori(ELSEWARE, Ltd.)
	Yutaka Murakami(M Create Co., Ltd.)

ISBN: 4-7661-1632-1
Printed and bound in China by Everbest Printing Co., Ltd.

HOW TO DRAW
MANGA
Computones
Vol. 4

Table of Contents

On the Techniques and Images Included and Introduced in this Book

Aside from a few exceptions, all of the original pieces in this book were created at a 600 dpi resolution in grayscale. Readers who will use the included CD-ROM and do their tone work on a computer are encouraged to do so on a machine that meets the indicated OS, CPU, memory, and hard disk requirements.

How to Use the Included CD-ROM

In order to use the included tone patterns CD-ROM, you must have at least one of the following software packages installed: Adobe Photoshop 5.0/5.5/6.0/7.0/CS or Adobe Photoshop LE 5.0; Adobe Photoshop Elements 1.0/2.0; Jasc Paint Shop Pro 7.0/8.0

Please use the CD-ROM after you have installed one of the above.

Romantic Tones

Tone is vital to romantic *manga*.

To those who wish to make their romantic *manga* more exciting or more dramatic, I highly recommend using tone. By applying various tone designs according to your preferences, you can portray a character's personality, a situation, or a scene that would be impossible using merely line drawings.

Manga Draft Rendered Solely as a Line Drawing

The simple addition of five types of tone dramatically transforms the composition.

Let's try playing around with tone a little. Here, all I did was select five types of common dot and gradation tones, and yet, if we compare this rendition to the line drawing on the left hand page, we see that it looks more like a proper romantic *manga*. By adding whichever tone that appealed to me to a few target locations, such as the hair, the clothing, and the shadows on the building, I was able to achieve this level of perfection.

Manga Draft Rendered Solely as a Tone Drawing

Revealing the Techniques of the Pros
Why Professional Manga Artists' Work Looks So Great

Here, we show you where and how a professional manga artist will apply tone. Adding a little variation and using tones to distinguish different composition parts produces impressive results.

❶ Haze Surrounding the Figure
Here, I used the Airbrush tool to etch the tone surrounding the figure. Softly blurring the edges allows you to add distinguishing features to the figure effectively.

❷ Hair
I used the highlight as a boundary, applying different tones to the regions above and below.

❸ Clothing Shadows
The scarf is folded and overlapping in areas. I applied tone to these interior regions to darken them and evoke a sense of volume.

❹ Skirt Pleats
Applying gradation tone in a fixed direction to the skirt's pleats established the direction of the pleats well as created a sense of volume.

❺ Tights
Here, I applied gradation tone moving in the direction of the thigh's center, where light is reflected. This allows me to portray the leg's curved surface.

❻ Accents
It is also great fun to use tone to create print patterns. Use a little ingenuity to come up with a unique look.

❼ Forests and Woods
Use different shades of tone to portray the heights of the different trees and a sense of distance. Use a darker shade for tall trees and a lighter one for short trees. Using only two levels to differentiate the trees still sufficiently evokes a sense of depth.

❽ Fabric Prints
Use random dot tone to generate the illusion of a gritty, sand-like texture when creating a distinctive print pattern or fabric.

❾ Facial Shadows
To make the face appear as a solid, apply tone to the hollows of the eyes, the sides of the nostrils, and underneath the nose. Other potential locations are the forehead and the cheekbone contours.

❿ On the Neck
This is a common place for applying tone to a figure. Adding tone to the neck to create shadow gives the face three-dimensionality, allowing the features to stand out.

Chapter 1

Simply Pasting on Tone for Easy-Peasy Romantic Couples

The Trick to Mastering Romance Manga Lies in Skillful Use of Backgrounds

Using Shading and Design to Create a Character's Image

The plots of romantic manga contain many lulls and climaxes, so portrayal of emotions is vital. Consequently, the artist will need to use tone in the background to create a sense of the character's emotional state when skilful rendition of the character alone will not suffice. Using the tone's shade to distinguish between light and shadow or opting for a different design pattern allows you to portray the character's mindset more appropriately.

Light-patterned Background Based in White

A white background tends to leave a rather vague impression on the viewer. By placing a light, patterned design on the background, you can give a character the impression of warmth.
Impressions Generated by White:
Gentle, graceful, light, sorrowful, and tender

High-Contrast Background Based in Black

Black backgrounds tighten up a panel and create a sense of tension. Adding a burst effect with black ground to an angular design expresses the seriousness of the character's emotional state.
Impressions Generated by Black:
Serious, earnest, worried, concentrating, a thought flitting through one's mind, etc.

How a Love Story Flows in Manga

1. Unrequited Love

This composition is portraying an indistinct feeling hidden in a character's heart. I selected a light design using primarily white.

2. Declaration of Love

Here, radiating lines and other effects capture the sense of tension felt in the moment that this love is confessed.

3. Mushy-Gushy Love

Using an attractive patterned tone or the like to suggest loving closeness makes the composition visually appealing.

4. Appearance of a Rival

Select a tone based primarily in black to suggest feelings of tension at having the love interest stolen away.

5. Break-up

Select a tone using primarily black to portray a dejected emotional state. Conversely, use a tone based in white to indicate a character is dumbstruck.

6. Happy Ending

Be sure to use the most garishly patterned tone you can find to build visually the sense of climax.

Shadows on Figures

Portraying Shadows on the Face

Make an effort to master adding shadows to human figures, as they constitute the basic element of manga. Humans have three-dimensional faces with peaks and valleys, and in manga facial features are consciously condensed to a certain number of points to which shading is added. Determine where to position the light source and plan how bright to make the light and how large the resulting shadow will be.

Hair
Create shadows for the hair overall or for discrete areas using tone.

From Cheek to Jaw
Create shadow following the cheekbone's contour. The trick here is to use a rounded form if the character is overweight or a straighter form if the character is thin.

On the Neck
Use shadows to create a contour line from the jaw to the collarbone. Shadows formed using tone make the facial features stand out, giving the face a sense of three-dimensionality.

Forehead
Create shadow for underneath the hair or for the upper regions of the forehead.

Eyes
Add shadows at strategic points: underneath the eyes and eyebrows and around the eyes..

Bridge of the Nose and Sides of the Nostrils
Shade along the bridge of the nose or the side of the nostril(s).

Underneath the Lips
Add a single shadow underneath the lips.

Applying Shadows for Different Light Intensities

Bright Lighting

In this composition, because light shines all over the face, the majority of the face remains white with shadows forming only at the forehead, the nose, and other strategic points.

Dim Lighting

In dim lighting, even those areas directly touched by light are not made bright. Rather, the composition is covered in shadowy, dark tones. Avoid applying uniform shades of tone. Use the tone to follow the cheekbone's contours, giving the face volume.

Shading the Body

Shadows typically form in depressed areas. Adding shadows to creases that form on garments when a character is wearing clothing allows you to suggest suppleness in the fabric or texture.

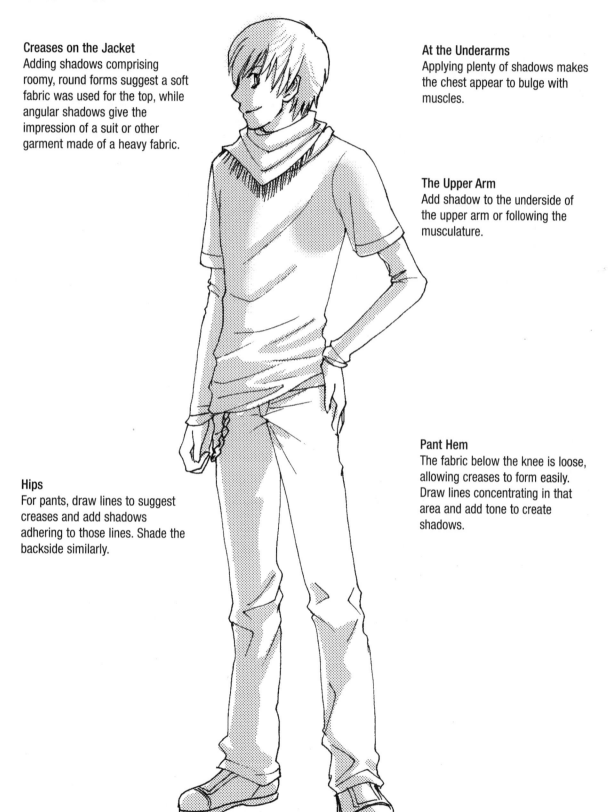

Creases on the Jacket
Adding shadows comprising roomy, round forms suggest a soft fabric was used for the top, while angular shadows give the impression of a suit or other garment made of a heavy fabric.

At the Underarms
Applying plenty of shadows makes the chest appear to bulge with muscles.

The Upper Arm
Add shadow to the underside of the upper arm or following the musculature.

Hips
For pants, draw lines to suggest creases and add shadows adhering to those lines. Shade the backside similarly.

Pant Hem
The fabric below the knee is loose, allowing creases to form easily. Draw lines concentrating in that area and add tone to create shadows.

Using Tone to Add Variation to a Composition

Using Gradation Tone

The viewer's perspective is not necessarily level with respect to a drawn figure. When drawing a composition with depth from either a high or low angle, use gradation tone to portray distance.

Assorted Gradation Tone Types

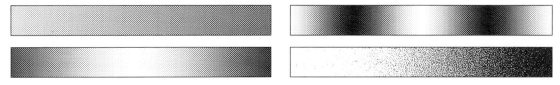

One-Point Perspective

When using tone to portray depth, usually objects close to the picture plane are made dark, and objects far from the picture plane are made light. However for rounded objects, parts close to the picture plane are rendered in white and parts far from the picture plane, in black.

High Angle

Here, gradation tone was added to the character's hair and clothing. Applying the tone so that the darker region faces up, while the tone becomes lighter as the eye travels down the leg, makes the girl's face appear larger.

Low Angle

Darken the underside of the feet and apply gradation tone so that it lightens as it approaches the top of the head. Apply gradation tone to the chest and thighs so that the regions close to the picture plane are white. This will create the illusion of a rounded surface.

Constructing a Composition in Perspective

Perspective is used to draw a panel that is more clearly composed from either a downward or upward-looking angle. Drawing in perspective is a technique whereby the artist selects a point of perspective (called the "vanishing point") and creates the illusion of depth based upon this perspective. Using this technique allows the artist to achieve a sense of depth or emphasize the size of an object.

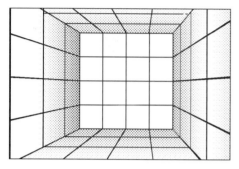

Conceiving Perspective

Pretend you are looking inside a square box. To make this easier for you to visualize, I drew a box. Notice how the far side of the box appears to narrow. Where do you think the vanishing point might be?

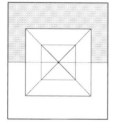

Here, the end of the road (the road as it disappears into the distance) was selected as the vanishing point, making the road appear to go on endlessly.

Two-Point Perspective

Well then, what if a composition were to have two vanishing points? For the answer, take a look at the figure provided. The building appears to jut out, giving the composition impact. Two-point perspective is popular for buildings' exteriors as well as interiors.

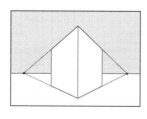

Lighting-Conscious Tone Work

Modifying Shadows According to the Light Source

Earlier, we discussed how the light's brightness affects the shadows' intensity. However, this depends on where the light source is positioned. By establishing that shadows will form and determining whether it is morning, afternoon, evening, or nighttime, you will find it easier to imagine the setting.

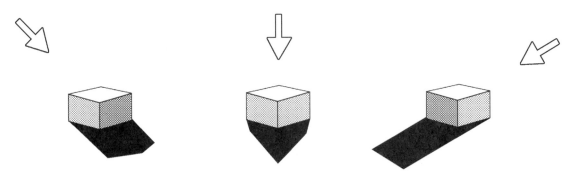

A shadow's shape and length changes according to where the light source is located. The light source is either above at an oblique angle, directly overhead, or to the side.

How Light Touches a Figure

Light Source at the Female Character's Side

Light Source

Here, both figures are bathed in light, and shadows form on sunken and protruding areas.

Light Source at the Male Character's Side

Light Source

The male character's shadow becomes elongated, and the female character becomes more enshrouded in shadow.

Overhead Light Source

Light Source

With the exception of the faces and chests, the characters are enshrouded in shadow.

Adding Dynamism

Using Speed and Radiating Lines

Artists use line tone to impart a sense of movement or dynamism on a human figure or other subject. How the artwork looks and the effects generated change according to whether the lines are applied in strategic locations or all over the composition.

Without Line Tone

With Line Tone

Using Speed Line-patterned Tone

Using Fine Lines
Here, I applied fine speed lines behind the character to evoke a sense of running and speed.

Increasing the Line Density
Here, I applied a tone with concentrated, fine speed lines to the background. This technique works well when you are trying to make motion appear more dramatic.

Using Thick Lines
Thicker lines make for a more dynamic portrayal. The final image may end up with a comedy manga feel, depending on the composition.

Radiating Lines

Artists use radiating lines when intending to attract attention to a figure, object, or other subject in a scene. Applying the tone centered on the target subject gives the composition impact. If the subject is moving, then radiating lines give it the feel of incredible speed. If the subject is still, then radiating lines suggest the moment when the camera lens zooms in on the subject.

Correct Example
The tone is centered on the figure.

Incorrect Example
The tone is shifted off-center.

Here, the use of radiating lines makes the scene appeared to have captured the moment the two characters embrace.

Speed Arcs

Here we have arced speed lines. These arcs are used similarly to speed lines, but they are able to portray circular motions not achievable using speed lines.

Use speed arcs to portray the moment a character looks back.

Using Patterned Tone to Dramatize a Scene

Use patterned tone to illustrate the gap between the expected and unexpected aspects of a character.

Placing an amusingly patterned tone in the background of a normally rendered scene allows you to lighten the atmosphere and soften the mood. This technique yields effective results in key humorous scenes or when adding such tone behind an otherwise serious character.

Using Patterned Tone to Transform a Character's Image
Here, the protagonist is designed to be a typical girl.

 USE TONE

Now, she's a bubblehead.
Here, I placed a protagonist with a pure, naive look about her against a patterned background. Looking at the composition, the incongruity of the fantastic nature of tone pattern juxtaposed against the girl's innocent smile gives us the impression that she is preparing some unimaginable dish.

 USE TONE

Juxtaposing a Straight-laced Character against Patterned Tone
Here, I added patterned tone behind a straight-laced girl, who is angry. The more serious the girl's expression, the more the humorous pattern stands out, making the girl's shock look funny.

Modes of Portrayal Using Other Tones

Large Dot Tone

Here, I am using dot tone as if it were patterned tone. Adding large dots to the background generates a fresh, modish look.

Thick Radiating Lines

Thick lines are better suited than fine lines to portraying a sense of vigor, might, and determination.

Tones with Rough Textures

Hatching tones, sand tones, and other tones with rough textures tend to darken the mood of a character or scene.

Etching Tone to Heighten Portrayal

Etching with the Brush

Etch and blur the dot tone to enhance its effects. Blurring the tone's edges and corners allows the tone to integrate into the composition and generate a sense of three-dimensionality.

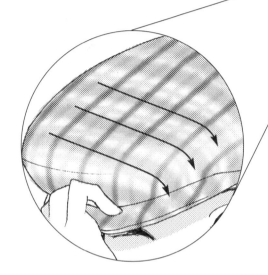

Here, I etched tone applied to the hat. By using numerous back and forth strokes, I was able to recreate the feel of soft wool. By not only blurring the tone, but doing so in regular intervals created the look of a design pattern.

Tip!

To etch tone, select either Eraser or Brush from the Tool Menu. Next, select white for the color. While maintaining awareness of the extent of the region you wish to etch, rub the tone's edges or areas of highlights using a stroking motion, gradually whitening and blurring the target areas.

Uses of the Airbrush

Handbag	Plastic	Hair

Etch the bag's edge to depict the leather's supple texture and rounded corners.

Softly etching the plastic film creates the illusion of reflected light.

Etching along the hair's locks to create blurred highlights produces a softened, natural look.

Adjusting the Brush's Size

Adjusting the brush size allows you to modify the width of the region blurred. Select various widths from the Brush Size tab and play around.

Wide Brush for Blurring

Narrow Brush for Blurring

Dither Brush

Tip! Using the Dither Brush

Select Dither Brush from the Brushes Palette. This will allow you to produce a scratchier style of etching. Layering etched strokes will produce a softer blur effect.

Widened Blurred Region

More Clearly Defined Blurred Region

Blurred Region with Sharply Delineated Borders

Playing Around with Different Brush Designs

How the Brush's Shape Affects the Resulting Image

Rather than sticking with the same brush you have used up to now, try experimenting with the various brushes loaded into your graphic software. The trick is to select a brush that produces a soft look. This will allow you to generate etching that is even softer than what you have been producing.

Brush Designs (Image from PhotoShop7.0)

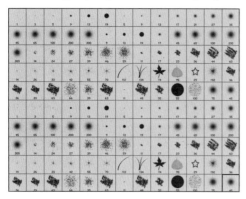

Etching Produced Using a Rounded Brush

Etching Produced Using a Stiff Brush

Etching Produced Using a Bristly Brush

Examples Showing Combinations of Different Brushes

Combining various different brush types when you etch allows you a wider range of expression.

Background: Produce cleanly defined etching using small dots.
Hat: Etch using a rounded brush.
String: Etch in using a small, coarse brush.
Flesh: Etch skin using a small, rounded brush.
Jacket: Etch roughly using a large, coarse brush with large dots.

Etching Tone to Create an Exciting Scene

Etch to create a soft blur and produce a faintly sad atmosphere.

Etch to softly blur around the figures, producing a scene with gentleness and warmth. This technique is popular in romance manga.

> **Tip!** Layering
>
> Use the layer function when intending to etch solely around a character and not the tone applied to the character itself. Select an additional layer from the Layers Palette, copy and paste a tone with the same pattern as the first layer, and etch where needed. Refer to your graphic software manual for more detail.

Etch the area surrounding a character to produce a softened image.
Use the technique to create the impression of fading emotions.

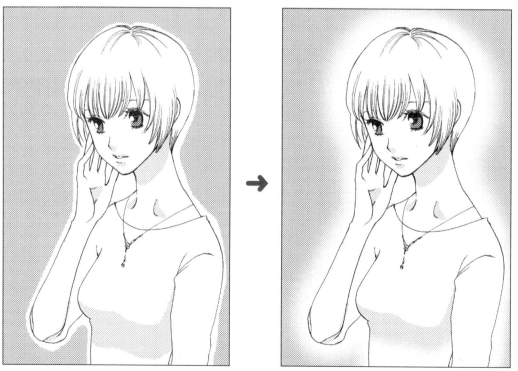

Softly etch the shadows on the flesh as well as the area surrounding the figure.
This will blend the figure with the background, making the character more appealing.

Impressions Affected by the Width and Darkness of the Etched Region

Blurring is not limited to that shown on the left page, but rather a versatile technique that can be applied in a wide range of situations. Let's take a look at a few more examples.

> **Tip!** Gradate the blurring for more effective results.
>
> Gradating the blur effect in much the same manner as gradated tone will yield more effective results.

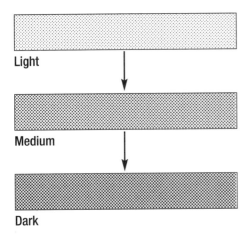

Light

Medium

Dark

Gradating the blurred etching used for the background yields a smoother, softer image.

Darken the background to produce a complicated atmosphere.

To suggest thorny emotions, such as seeds of doubt or anxiety, use black fill on the background to create a dark mood. Then etch around the character to create a blurred effect.

Rendering a Love Story in Tone

Selecting Tone Suitable to Romance Manga

Use tone to portray the stages leading from the initial meeting to the declaration of love. The tone does not function as the background but rather to recreate adroitly the thrill experienced by the couple.

Stages Leading to the Declaration

Striking up a Conversation   At a Loss for Words   Love Is Declared!

Stage 1: Use radiating lines for when one strikes up a conversation with the other.

Confessing one's feelings is a very brave act. It constitutes an anxious moment for the confessor. Radiating lines lend themselves well to eliciting a sense of tension

The key point regarding radiating lines lies in using them for the moment that the two meet or the moment that love is confessed.

Stage 2: Use fantastic patterned tone to portray heart-thumping scenes of the two gazing lovingly at one another.

This scene illustrates the moment that one has revealed feelings of love and now awaits a response from the other. Complicated emotions flit through each of their minds, meaning that a design showing a flash of a thought works well.

The more serious the expression on the character's face, the more a bright tone pattern will serve to illustrate the girl's innocent feelings.

Stage 3: Use dot tone to portray the sense of nervousness at having daringly confessed her love.

Applying dot tone to the entirety of the face rather than to the background creates the illusion of blushing in embarrassment. Furthermore, darkening the background suggests dark, melancholic emotions.

Portraying Couples in Love

Using Sunshine

Use the warmth of sunlight to soften the look of the couple. Let's take a look at the effects of soft versus hard, delineated etching of the tone surrounding the characters.

Image in Soft Light

Here, the brush was used to blur the tone surrounding the characters. The key points in selecting the brush are that brushes with bristles that are round like a lint pill and with space between the bristles will leave clean etched strokes on the tone.

Brush image

Image with a Clearly Delineated Light Effect

Here, rays of light were created to reproduce the feeling of warm sunlight. Select either a brush with a fine point and carefully draw a straight line or select a small, rounded brush and draw a straight line.

Brush image

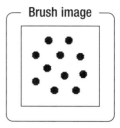

The use of light and shadow draws out the figures.

Add tone to underneath the characters' faces to darken them. This will make the faces stand out further, drawing the viewer's eyes to them.

Portraying Figures from the Rear

Add a substantial amount of tone to create shadow on characters looking back. Use the brush to blur the tone's borders. Take note that applying too much tone to the flesh could just make it appear dirty.

Using the Silhouette

Using black fill on the characters will make the intimacy between the two more vivid.

Breakup Scenes: Portraying Shock

Using Black to Seal That Sense of Surprise

When expressing surprise in a work of manga, select either a dark palette or black fill to give the panel visual impact. The trick lies in darkening the overall palette. The darker the tone, the more dejected the character's psychological state will seem.

Line Drawing and Tone   Line Drawing and Tone   Line Drawing, Tone, and Solid
                                                              Black Fill

Etching to Achieve a Realistic Rendition

Going that extra step and etching the tone will allow you to convey to the reader a sense of extreme surprise. Use a little ingenuity when adding shadow position the light source either high or low in the composition to a location where shadows would form in abundance.

Using Tone to Portray a Scream, a Fierce Grudge, or Despair

Use line tone in lieu of a dark shade of tone to imbue dynamism on a panel focusing on a character's emotional state. Try line tone for unadulterated fury, rain-like lines for anger, and speed arcs for anguish.

Furious Yell

Use line tone to portray pure fury. Layering lined tone is another viable option.

Rancor

Line tone that is reminiscent of rain works well when trying to achieve a spine-chilling mood.

Scream

Use speed arcs to portray a psychological state of torment, anguish or the like, that might make the character's body writhe.

Getting Back Together and the Conclusion

Close-Ups and Long Angles in Perspective

When showing two characters, avoid lining up the pair. Instead, draw the composition in perspective, using the positioning of the characters and a sense of distance to achieve more visually effective results. Use a close-up to achieve a more intimate composition and a long angle for a more expositionary panel.

Close-Ups

Overhead angles afford a greater sense of intimacy when composing scenes where the couple is snuggled close. Select somewhere beneath the pair's feet as the vanishing point and use foreshortening, drawing the heads proportionally large.

Long Angles

Use long angled compositions in perspective to show one character calling out to another over a great distance. Position the vanishing point according to the direction of the character's gaze, and ensure that you do not draw the panel's components to be awkwardly large.

Drawing a Background That Emphasizes the Mood

When intending to express a particular atmosphere in a scene, use a long angled panel that illustrates the scenery or situation in which the character is positioned.

The Couple in a Park

The Couple Indoor

The Couple at the Beach

The Couple on Top of a Hill

The Couple by the Riverside

Tricks to Applying Tone

The following are basic points of consideration in applying tone successfully.
Ensure that you make effective use of tone.

Point 1: Distinguishing Use of Different Degrees of Darkness

When using multiple tones, avoid using tones of the same density (i.e. darkness) in order to give the composition three-dimensionality. Use light tone for shadow in areas touched by light and dark tone for areas far from the picture plane.

Point 2: Distinguishing the Appearances of the Different Subject Matter

Selecting tones with different patterns, such as dot tone with sand tone or hatching tone for a top and pants or a top and skirt combination, is an effective way to handle using multiple tones on clothing and other components.

Point 3: Distinguishing Tone Patterns

Using patterned tones with distinctive designs intended to attract the eye can result in a cluttered image when these tones are laid side by side. Avoid layering such tones as much as reasonable. Select a patterned tone for either the top or bottom of a character's outfit, but not for both.

Point 4: *Sujikezuri* Effects

"*Sujikezuri* " is the etching of the tone's borders. Moderately etching the borders of tone applied to clothing, etc. suggests light around the edges of the garment, resulting in a more naturalistic portrayal.

Chapter 2

Portraying Characters and Dramatization Techniques

Creating Facial Expressions

Combining Tone and Etching to Portray a Smiling Face

When intending to create a fetching face, center the face on the tone when you apply it. Applying tone to the cheeks and to the hair is a popular means of accentuating a flushed look to the face.

Face Rendered as a Line Drawing

With tone added to the hair, the facial expression takes on a realistic appearance.

Tip!
Achieving More Daring Renditions

Applying tone to the face overall and then blurring around the form to achieve a soft look enhances the sense of embarrassment.

Layering line tone to suggest luster in the hair or flushed cheeks gives the face a more natural look.

Mastering the Embarrassed Face

Give careful consideration to the effects and dramatization techniques you will need to adopt to make a character appear embarrassed or enticing. Enhancing the facial expression or heightening the sense of endearment has the potential to change completely the intensity of the reader's emotional involvement.

Embarrassed Face

Add diagonal lines (i.e. hatching) to the cheeks, apply tone to the face overall, and etch the surrounding area with the blur brush to achieve a softened effect.

Laughing Face

Adjust the thickness and angle of the lines applied to the cheeks. You might also consider applying tone to the cheeks as an accent.

Smiling Face

Using finely etched strokes on the tone applied to the face and the region surrounding the background yields a soft expression and mood.

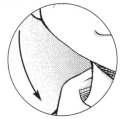

Creating Facial Expressions (Cont.)

Angry Face

Deep furrows in the brow and wrinkles from the eyes to the mouth constitute identifying elements of an angry face. Try overlapping two tones to produce a more intense facial expression.

Tip!
Overlapping Tone

Layering tones is a snap if you use the layer function. Call up the Layers Palette display, select New/Add Layer and apply over the previous layer.

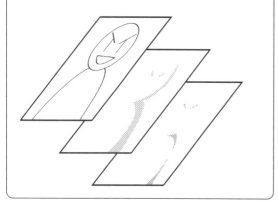

Face as a Line Drawing

Here, wrinkles in the face are drawn, and the expression does not come across as angry.

Face with Single Layer of Tone

Here, tone has been applied to the shadows and the wrinkles, creating a sense of three-dimensionality.

Face with Two Layers of Tone

By applying two layers of tone between the eyes and at the wrinkles around the mouth, making the expression seem truly harried and angry. When to accentuate a facial expression, adding shadows not normally allows you to achieve more effective results.

Modulating the Degree of Overlap to Enhance the Facial Expression

The appearance or impression projected changes according to how two layers of dot tone are overlapped. The more the two layers are shifted, the darker the layered region appears. Consequently, I recommend that you play around with the tone to see for yourself how the layered tone appears in different degrees of overlap.

Two Layers Shifted Slightly

Two Layers Shifted Halfway

Two Layers Shifted Until There Is No Overlap of the Dots of Either Tone

Portraying Clothing Fabric Textures

Fashion constitutes an important technique the artist uses to portray a character's individuality. Give careful consideration to the material and shape of the fabric used and use tone to portray its texture.

Street Clothes

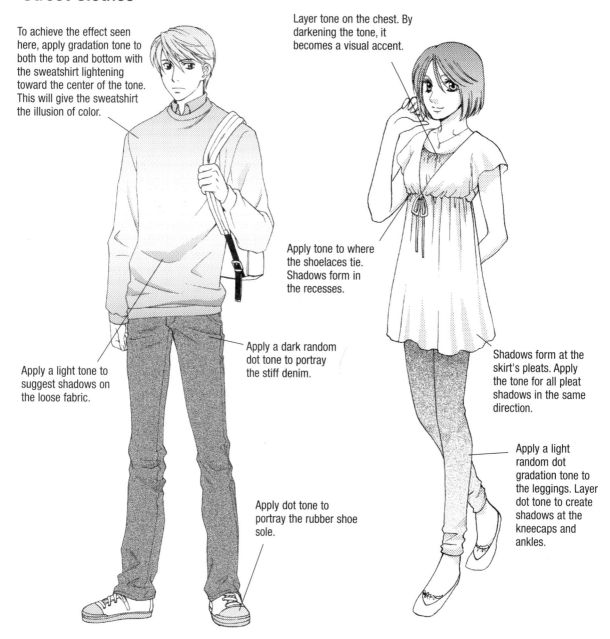

To achieve the effect seen here, apply gradation tone to both the top and bottom with the sweatshirt lightening toward the center of the tone. This will give the sweatshirt the illusion of color.

Apply a light tone to suggest shadows on the loose fabric.

Apply a dark random dot tone to portray the stiff denim.

Apply dot tone to portray the rubber shoe sole.

Layer tone on the chest. By darkening the tone, it becomes a visual accent.

Apply tone to where the shoelaces tie. Shadows form in the recesses.

Shadows form at the skirt's pleats. Apply the tone for all pleat shadows in the same direction.

Apply a light random dot gradation tone to the leggings. Layer dot tone to create shadows at the kneecaps and ankles.

Male Character

Here we see a character dressed casually in a sweatshirt and jeans. Distinguish between the two fabrics by portraying denim as a stiff, rough fabric, while adding shadows to portray the suppleness of the sweatshirt's fabric.

Female Character

This character is wearing a see-through blouse and snug leggings. Add shadows to the blouse to portray the ruffles and gradation tone to the leggings to make the legs appear slim.

Tip!
The Inside of a Woman's Purse

Apply tone to the various personal affects located in the purse. A quick material solution would be to apply gradation tone to suggest the shiny, lustrous finish of vinyl or leather. Conversely, add random dot tone or hatched tone to reproduce the texture of a bumpy or rough surface.

On a Date

Here, I dressed the figure in a hunting hat and scarf and then added patterned tone to add a touch of accent to her outfit. Making the patterned tone's print size vary for the cap versus the scarf gives the character a pleasing appearance.

I darkened the jacket by layering tones to evoke the sense of a heavy fabric.

I applied gradation tone to the long hair in order to accentuate its length.

The cardigan in this image is plain, so I selected a dark dot tone for the shell to balance the figure.

As with the hair, I applied gradation tone to the long skirt in order to emphasize its length.

Again, we see jeans, but here I used a light random dot tone. I also applied dot tone to the side shadows, creating the illusion of volume.

The jacket's color is dark overall, so for this image I selected a light colored tone for the pants to balance the figure.

Apply tone according to the tonal impression projected by the color. To portray the shadows, apply layered dot tone from the tip of the toe across the foot's side.

Male Character

Here, I decided to add a patterned tone on top of a hat, scarf, and other accessories for a more ostentatious composition.

Female Character

Adding a cap and dressing her in boots instead of regular shoes establishes a difference between this outfit and everyday wear. Apply tone to clothing for a classier looking effect.

Formal Western Dress

Dot tones of 30% density or greater are commonly used for tuxedos with tailcoats and other formalwear. Attach the tone as a solid fill and avoid etching with the brush.

Because I had applied to the garments overall, creating a dark palette, I made a point of omitting tone on the hair on this figure. If you were to apply tone in such a case, I suggest opting for a light tone.

Here, I applied gradation tone to the hair, while envisioning a large, fluffy hairdo. I darkened the ends of the hair and lightened the top to achieve a buoyant feel.

Use a random dot tone or any alternative pattern other than a standard dot tone on the vest underneath the jacket. This will establish a difference with the jacket.

By not applying tone to the cape's armholes, I am able to emphasize the fabric's whiteness and create the illusion of sheerness.

For this character, I applied gradation tone to the dress so that it darkened as the eye travels down., making the figure appear slender.

Apply a dot tone that is one shade darker than the garment to portray crease shadows, etc.

Creating shadows that fall across the buttocks accentuates the figure underneath.

Male Character

Tuxedos and other essential formalwear tend to feature primarily dark shades, which require the use of dark tones. Give consideration to overall balance and pay attention to the shades of other tones in the composition when applying tone to formalwear.

Female Character

Silk and other luxury fabrics with a sheen are used in women's formalwear. Be sure to use gradation tone with women's formal wear, including the accessories, in order to recreate the look of glossy textures.

Formal Japanese Dress

A modest pattern is woven into the garment worn underneath the outer robes, so opt for a random dot or hatched tone.

Shade the inside of the sleeve using black fill. This will give the kimono a sophisticated feel where black becomes the primary color.

Add shading to the chest to achieve a three-dimensional effect.

Lustrous fabrics are frequently used for obi (sashes), which wrap around the waist. With the brush, produce softly etched, blurring strokes down the center of the obi to create a shiny, highlight effect.

Embellish the hips and cuffs with a decorative pattern to achieve an ornate look.

Use two layers of tone to achieve well-defined shadows for rolls and turns in the fabric. Darkening the tone gives the fabric a sense of volume.

The footwear is also decorated with a modest woven pattern. Pay attention to achieving a visual balance, and select a lighter shade of tone than that used on the outer robe

Adding a decorative pattern to the feet would give the figure overall visual balance, stabilizing the image.

Male Character

This type of dress is called a "haori hakama" and represents the most common of traditional Japanese formalwear. The palette consists of black and other somber colors.

Female Character

This type of kimono is called a "furisode" and is worn to wedding ceremonies or visits to shrines and other such formal occasions. The silk of a furisode is typically decorated with flower or animal designs and a colorful palette.

Portraying Male vs. Female Characters Actions

Poses for Characters in Love

There are several stock poses used to depict a character's psyche in romance manga. Make an effort to use tone and shading when rendering these poses.

For this type of composition, avoid adding tone to the character or background. Instead, apply tone solely to the passersby. Use contrasting tones to generate the mood of a lone character within a crowd, waiting.

Here, I applied tone to the overall composition and then etched around the main character. This made the panel appear as if a camera lens were focusing on the figure, projecting the atmosphere of an individual buried within the throng.

Portraying Shifts in Facial Expressions

When depicting lonely scenes where a character awaits a lover, render the overall composition in dark shades to generate a forlorn atmosphere.

When the lover finally arrives, switch abruptly to white as the primary color to brighten and enliven the image.

Interior Scenes

As with outdoor scenes, use shading with interior scenes to project a forlorn atmosphere. Incorporate props to create the mood.

In scenes of a lone character waiting at a table, use a long angle to show the character facing a vacant chair, thereby painting an atmosphere of emptiness.

Likewise, when portraying a scene of a character alone at a table, positioning a teacup or other dish in the center of focus causes the viewer to have associations with loneliness.

Again, use white to brighten scenes where the awaited lover finally arrives. Applying a cheerful, patterned tone around the subject also proves effective for lightening the atmosphere.

Poses of Two Characters Side-by-Side

Shading Figures Touching

Poses where two characters touch are crucial to date scenes. Methods of shading change when the two characters are side by side, which means that the beginning artist will need to master basic figure portrayal.

Conceiving of Two Figures Touching as a Solid

You will find it easier to conceive of how shadows form on two close figures by imagining the body parts as solids. Shadows tend not to be visible on overlapping parts, increasing the area of reflected light overall.

Here we see two figures standing side by side normally.

Face Close-up of Two Characters Side by Side

Heighten the Degree of Closeness to Underscore Intimacy

When showing two figures touching, visualize the pose first in the form of two intertwined manikins to facilitate the drawing process. Using manikins as a model will give you an idea of how to portray the figures as solids and how shadows form.

Here we see a male and female character with arms interlocked and a light source located to the left.

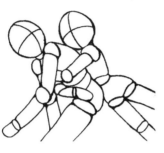

In this image, the female character is on top of the male character with the light source overhead.

Tone Work on Breaking Up Scenes

Using Cleanly Defined Etched Strokes to Portray Sorrow

When rendering melancholy in a breakup scene, rather than merely drawing the face of a character crying, apply tone etched with clearly defined strokes for a more effective look.

> **Tip!** How to Etch Straight Lines
>
> Select a small brush to etch. Since the mouse makes it difficult to draw in a straight line, use a tablet if one is available. Place a straightedge on the tablet and then draw the line to produce a cleanly etched stroke.

Make an effort to show the disparate emotional states in the male character, who just broke off the relationship, and the female character, who was just dumped. Try to dramatize the scene to convey a sense of her shock.

Including the Background in the Dramatization of a Memorable Breakup Scene

Breakup Scene underneath a Streetlight

This panel shows the couple breaking up in front of the female character's house late at night. To create such scenes, apply dark tones to the background in general, including the house and light tones on the female character. The difference in shades creates the illusion that the girl is bathed in light from the streetlamp. Be sure to etch the tone at the female character's feet.

In close-ups, add tone to the background as called for by the scene. In the case of the panel to the right, because the female character was lit from behind by the streetlight, I applied gradation tone.

Breakup Scene against the Glow of Sunset

Sunsets create striking scenes. Apply gradation tone to both the sky and the ocean in the background, and add clearly defined etchings to where the clouds and setting sun are echoed on the water. Conversely, avoid applying tone to the figures. Instead, use white ground to make them stand out.

Portraying and Dramatizing the Figures

Using a Rounded Brush to Create Rounded Forms

Use rounded forms on key areas to make the female character's body appear more attractive. Add shading to the figure's hills and valleys and then etch the shadows. This will produce an appealing silhouette where roundness is accentuated.

Maintain awareness of where the figure curves, having it taper at the waist from the underarm and etching around the shadows formed on the chest.

Draw the back subtly arced and etch shadows on the back to achieve enticing results.

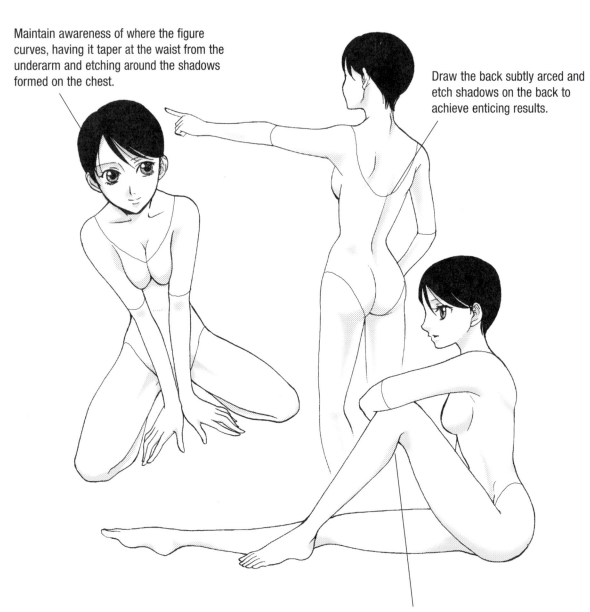

Depict the thigh of the leg the girl is hugging as a solid object. Etch to blur softly the shadow on the underside of the posterior and knee.

In order to render a body on the whole using round forms, first add pale shadows around the outside of the figure. Next, etch to blur the edges.

Apply tone to the inside of the skirt to suggest shadow. Etching along the thigh muscles creates an alluring image.

Apply tone to those areas in shadow on the inside of the figure and etch the corners of any forms that should be rounded.

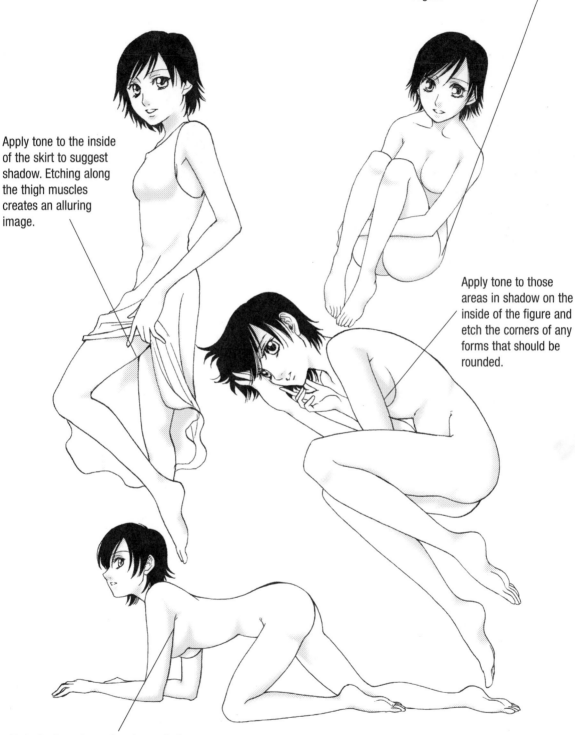

Etch shadows formed underneath the figure according to the figure's silhouette shape. Etching along curved contours will allow you to generate the appropriate look.

Portraying Love Using Tone for Various Couples

High School Couple (Teens)

Here we have a couple overflowing with youth. Exaggerating the characters' youthfulness will yield more satisfying results.

Point 1 Figure Drawing

In order to create a juvenile or infantile face, increase the proportion of the face occupied by the eyes (i.e. make the eyes bigger).

Point 2 Portraying the Overall Form

- Use the same shade of tone for the necktie and bow.
- The jackets, pants, and skirts are typically plain, but with different shades of tone used for the top and bottom.
- The socks are normally plain white or navy.
- The shoes are typically black leather loafers.

Point 3

Portraying the Couple on a Date

Depict a couple brimming with youth. I recommend using a flamboyant pattern or a pattern with a fantastic sensibility in the background.

Adult Couple (Twenties)

The two shown here are already adult members of society. They both hold high hopes regarding the future, so their eyes are shown sparkling brightly.

Point 1 **Figure Drawing**

The faces' basic silhouette is not much different from the characters in their teens. Here, I gave the male character glasses to project a more mature air. For the female character, I drew her with a perm to make her appear older.

When drawing long hair, add gradation tone to generate a sense of volume.

Point 2 **Portraying the Overall Form**

- A print or checked tone is used for the necktie.
- A dark tone is used for the suit to give the fabric volume.
- Use gradation tone to portray the sparkle on diamonds and other glittering jewelry.
- The man typically wears leather shoes, while the woman wears pumps or boots. Apply gradation tone to create a gloss.

Point 3

Portraying the Couple on a Date

Project an energetic atmosphere appropriate to the characters' personalities. When shifting scenes and moving into a romantic setting or the like, play around with different tones in the background and try to find a tone that matches the mood.

Middle-aged Couple (Forties)

Here we have a pair of an age where they could be someone's parents. Portray both characters projecting a composed, sophisticated air and demeanor.

Point 1 Figure Drawing

When drawing characters that span from youth to middle-age, raise the position of the eyes relative to that of characters in their teens. Render facial shadows using relatively straight contours, and when etching, use clearly defined forms. Add wrinkles around the eyes and mouth of the female character.

Point 2 Portraying the Overall Form

- For the man's suit, feel free to opt for a patterned tone.
- Since you are suggesting white hair, the tone is not etched.
- If you have used a print for the suit, then select black for the shoes to achieve a sophisticated look.
- Accessorize by giving the male character a tiepin and the female character jewelry with large diamonds, opals, or other gems.

Point 3

Portraying the Couple on a Date

A darkish tone in the background gives the scene a sophisticated look. However, this generation is not without its flamboyance, so design the date to take place at a ritzy hotel or restaurant, and create a glamorous scene.

Elderly Couple (Seventies)

Here we have a senior citizen couple. Draw the characters with downward sloping eyes to create a cheerful expression and upward slanting eyes to portray a mulish attitude. You will find the characters easier to draw if you consider what type of personality the character will have.

Point 1 **Figure Drawing**

Overall figures sport plenty of wrinkles and creases with flesh and fabric hanging down. Reduce the amount of space you will allot to using tone to portray shadows and make the forms more angular. Adding tone to the eyes, mouth, and cheekbones works well for rendering these features.

Point 2 **Portraying the Overall Form**

- Design the clothing to appear warm and with a plain print. Random dot tone is an effective choice for portraying stiff fabrics.
- Give the female figure personal effects. Show her wearing a scarf around her neck or a shawl draped over her shoulders using patterned tone for the design.
- Show one or both characters holding a woodgrain cane. Dot tone works well. If you intend to create a pattern, opt for a random dot tone or a hatched tone.

Point 3

Portraying the Couple on a Date

Soften the image by gently blurring the tone, thereby projecting a tender atmosphere. Depending on the nature of the story, selecting a patterned tone with a fantasy theme could give the composition a humorous touch.

Male (Homosexual) Couple

In couples comprising two males, we still find one partner taking on a masculine, active role and the other a more feminine, passive role. Be sure to clarify the differences in the character's personalities and their rank within the relationship when you draw them.

Point 1 Figure Drawing

Give the active character clearly defined features, while using fine lines for the passive character, painting the picture of a sensitive individual. Drawing the two characters with different hairstyles, eyes of different sizes, and jaw lines of different shapes will distinguish them as well.

Point 2 Portraying the Overall Form

- Select a suit or other formal-looking dress for the active character in order to paint him as a serious, yet sexy personality. In contrast, draw plenty of creases on the passive character's shirt, and imbuing him with a rumpled, careless sexiness.
- Use similar accessories and jewelry to what you might give a female character such as pierced earrings or custom-designed rings to expand the image. Use primarily gradation tone to render silver jewelry.

Key Points in Portraying the Couple on a Date

Exploit the incongruence in the two characters' worldliness and add a gaudy tone to the background for a humorous effect or apply a dark gradation tone or hatching tone to create a serious mood.

Chapter 3

Dramatizing and Rendering Scenes

Portraying Love Scenes

The Couple Nestling Close

There are various poses showing couples snuggling close. Make an effort to learn tone work and compositional techniques.

Point!
Here we have a pose composed in perspective from a moderate high angle. Apply gradation tone to the clothing as well in order to achieve a sense of depth.

Point!
Since the two are standing side by side, avoid applying too much tone for shading. Instead, apply the minimum possible to give the composition a sense of three-dimensionality.

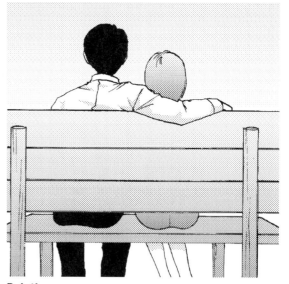

Point!
Position the two figures close together so as to create a triangular composition. Create a tender atmosphere by applying tone to the background and softly blurring the edges.

Point!
Note that even from a rear view, the female character's legs are still positioned in a direction to form a triangular composition.

Point!
Tone covers most of the composition. Etching the flowing clouds and the sparkling water's surface with the Blur Brush to create highlights allows you to project a sunny atmosphere.

Point!
Apply a light tone to suggest sunlight streaming through the trees, adding sunrays here and there to achieve an impressive panel.

Portraying Love Scenes (Cont.)

Portraying Couples Embracing

Next, we discuss tone work and compositional techniques for portraying two characters embracing.

Point!

When composing scenes where two characters gaze at one another, have the male character pull in his chin to look down and show the female character arcing her back slightly and looking up. Note that the forms of the neck's shadows change according to where the light source is positioned.

Point!

In compositions where a male character embraces a female character from behind, draw the male character's body at a moderate diagonal, picturing an inverted, narrow triangle. Be sure to include the creases formed in the clothing as a result of the wrapped arms.

Point!

Drawing twisting figures is not an easy feat. When creating such a composition, divide the female figure's upper body into two parts: the chest and the abdomen. This will facilitate the process.

Tip! Portraying Hands

Scenes of two characters embracing seem all the more vivid when the woman's distinctively soft hands are properly rendered.

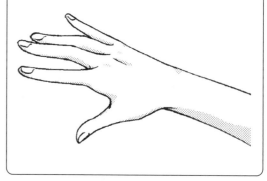

Point!
When composing a key scene, take extra care with the background, which offers information toward the setting in which the two characters are placed. Use a dark palette combined with brightly shining light to achieve a memorable composition.

Point!
Draw a female character flying at lover with her back arced. Including plenty of shadows with the creases formed on her back following the body's contours will give the figure momentum.

Kissing Scenes

On the following pages we discuss tone work and poses for kissing scenes—an indispensable element of romance manga.

Commonly in kiss scenes, we find a taller male character embracing a female character, so that he has to hunch forward. Create an abundance of shadows for the clothing creases on his jacket's chest. This will give his forward-leaning pose a more natural feel.

Apply tone to the mouth to shade. This will give the connecting lips a sense of three-dimensionality. Add shadows to the neck underneath the chin. Gently blur the edges of shadows on the female character to soften the image.

Feathery Kiss

For this kiss, imagine the lips lightly brushing against one another. Experiment with the lips shapes. Draw them in their pristine form, or show the lips smiling or pouting. Apply tone to give the lips volume.

Gentle Peck

Step 1: Center Point Positioning and Tone Selection

Step 2: Applying Tone and Solid Black

This is a quick, unexpected kiss or a light kiss given as an expression of love. Draw the characters' facial expressions and add tone for the appropriate shadows. You can further enhance the mood by applying tone that suits the setting to the background.

Deep Kiss

Apply light tones to each the mouths and tongues to create a heavy scene.

The figures are pressed together in a greater degree of contact for the Deep kiss than they are in regular kiss scenes. Emphasize the figures' contours. Add shadows to the musculature of the arms and legs to create the feel of two people enthusiastically pulling each other close.

Tip! Portraying Lips

Giving the female character's lips a sense of volume accentuates the sensuality of a kiss scene. Apply gradation tone to darken the lower lip and use clearly defined etched strokes to create highlights if the character is supposed to be wearing lipstick or lip-gloss.

Portraying Lovemaking Scenes

Using Sheet Rumpling and Wrinkles to Portray Lovemaking

The lovemaking scene constitutes the primary climax of romance manga. Use the bed linens and bedspread or quilt to depict the characters' psychological states effectively, the bed linen and cover.

Using Lumps in the Bedcover to Suggest a Lovemaking Scene

When drawing characters wrapped in a bedspread, imagine the figures underneath the bedspread when you draw.

Bedcover Textures

Produce a line drawing of the undulations in the bed sheets, and apply tone to create shadows in any recessed areas. Etch, generating a soft, blurred effect around the shadows' edges to reproduce the fabric's supple texture. Etch to blur in a wide area those shadows of particularly rounded forms.

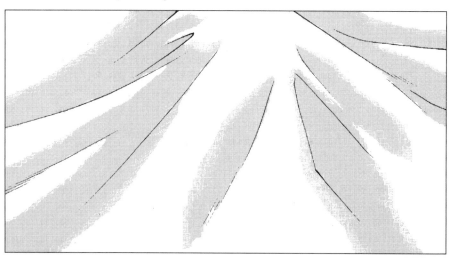

Area Where a Wide Patch of Tone is Etched to Blur

Assorted Bedcovers

To portray a scene where a figure is wrapped in bed sheets, use plenty of tone to create shadow and add an abundance of rumples and wrinkles to achieve a charming image.

Add plenty of highlights around bedspread where it covers the mouth in scenes where a character shyly hides her mouth with the bedspread. Adding sunken rumples around the target area makes the image even more convincing.

When producing a composition where a character grabs the sheet with his or her hand, add plenty of small shadows to the rumpled fabric to create a wrinkled look.

Using Sheets to Suggest Sadness

Create a large shadow in the center of the sheet to suggest that someone had been sleeping there who is now gone. Add rippled shadows, adhering to the crumpling of the sheet.

Creating Backgrounds from Photos

Using a Photocopier to Process Photographs

Artists often have the opportunity to use images from newspapers, magazines, and photographs in the backgrounds of manga panels, maintaining the subject matter as it appears in the original image. On this page, we discuss using a photocopier to reproduce the original photograph any number of times and then scanning it as well as tracing the image to the background.

Here we see a source photograph. Make an effort to collect on a daily basis clippings from newspapers and magazines, whenever you find an image you feel would be appropriate to use as source material for backgrounds.

This is a line drawing derived from the photograph. Normally, you would lay manga draft paper over the photograph and trace.

Imaginary Backgrounds Produced Using a Photocopier and Production Techniques

Let's take a look at the effects of repetitious photocopying.

First Generation Photocopy: The image is slightly blurred.

Second Generation Photocopy: The image can be just barely distinguished by looking at the building outlines.

Third Generation Photocopy: All outlines and contours are indistinguishable except for solid black areas.

Applying and Etching Images

Layered Images

Lay a drawing of the character over the photocopied image.

Applying Cloud Tone

Carefully erase any extraneous lines extending beyond the actual representation of the character itself and add cloud tone to the sky.

Blurring Architectural Structures

Use a large brush to blur the edges and use repeated back and forth strokes to etch the buildings and the trees close to the picture plane. Once the building seems integrated with the character drawing, the process is finished.

Using Tone to Portray Date Spots

The Out-of-Doors

Park at Night

The composition takes a dark tone overall. Using a solid tone would bury the scene is utter darkness, so apply gradation tone to the ground and each tree to generate a little brightness.

Tip!
Bench Tone Work

Use a different tone for the bench's woodgrain planks and frame. When intending to accentuate the woodgrain, opt for a random dot tone. Etch the planks' corners with the pencil tool or with a fine brush to achieve a worn and weathered look.

Amusement Park

Portray the neon lights and the texture of the gigantic steel frame. Select a blur brush that will allow you to create dry, light etched strokes, and etch each of the Ferris wheel's seats to suggest neon lights.

Next, select a brush that will allow you to create clearly defined etched strokes and etch the tone, visualizing tiny scratches on the corners of the steel frame.

Boating Lake

The key here lies in portrayal of the water's surface. Before applying tone and while you are still at the under drawing stage, sketch shadows around the water's edge and shadows of people reflected on the water's surface.
Next, apply gradation tone.
Select a brush that will allow you to produce clearly defined, etched strokes and etch as if drawing ripples.
This will create reflections on the water's surface.

Interiors

Cafe

Artists frequently draw cafes as rendezvous venues. Apply tone to the floor, the walls, the tables, and other interior elements. Avoid using too many different tones. The trick here is to limit yourself to three shades of tone or to use a gradation tone. Etch the light reflection on the windowpane to create a softly blurred effect.

Tip!
Upholstered Chair Tone Work

Apply dot or gradation tone, envisioning a leather-upholstered chair. Softly etch to blur the rounded corners, creating the look of a glossy shine on the leather.

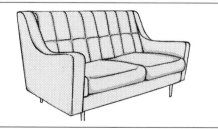

Bar

Use dark shades to create the appropriate atmosphere. Select a dark tone and apply it to the ceiling and regions far from the picture plane. Draw the lighting fixtures and etch with a rounded brush to suggest light.

Cinema

The screen constitutes the sole light source inside the dark movie theater. Add highlights only to the upper portion of the seat backs, which face the light source. Apply progressively darkening tone to the rear of the seats, applying either a dot or gradation tone.

Vehicles

Motorcycles

The key to achieving a sense of three-dimensionality lies in portraying the fairing's curved surface. Apply a different shade of tone to each of the frame, the wheels, and the windshield. Add light reflections to the windshield by etching with a rounded brush.

Tip!
Helmet Tone Work

To execute the tone work for the round helmet, apply either dot or gradation tone to the form overall. Next, add highlights to the helmet's upper portions. I recommend etching the groove as well, double-checking the position of the light source as you etch.

Roller Coasters

Apply speed lines or other lined tone to achieve a sense of velocity. Etch to create highlights on the roller coaster's angular body. Again, use the Brush tool to etch, so that the stroke moves toward the back of the coaster. This will enhance the sense of speed.

Jet Ski

Apply different tones to each surface forming the body to project a sense of three-dimensionality. Add gradation tone to the water's surface. You might either etch with a rounded blur brush to create water spray or use the Eraser tool to rub the tone, creating a matte finish that suggests billowing smoke.

Seasonal Date Spots

Summer: Swimming Pool

Undulation of waves forms a key point in representation. Apply gradation tone to the overall pool. Next, select a brush that produces rough strokes and use a motion as if you were drawing hills. Use quick strokes for portions of tone near the picture plane and solid, continuous strokes for portions far from the picture plane, establishing a difference in shade between the two.

Tip!
Inner Tube Tone Work

Select either a dot tone or a gradation tone in order to portray the texture of vinyl. Overlap the upper half with a layer of tone, shifting the upper layer slightly to create a darker shade. Finish by using the Blur Brush to etch lines down the inner tube's center to create highlights.

Summer: Waterslide

As with the Jet Ski, lay speed lines over the dot tone applied to the background. This will generate a sense of velocity. Etch both the back and front of the inner tube using the Eraser tool to create the look of spraying mist.

Summer: Hiking

The key point here lies in sunlight bathing down on the scene. Apply dot tone to the overall background or cloud-patterned tone to the sky. Once you have finished the preparatory work, select a small brush and etch sunbeams using a downward motion and straight strokes.

Tone Work Tricks for Drawing Couples

Four Key Points

1. Be selective about shading.
Narrow shading on the face down to key areas and use simple forms. Conversely, add shadows to creases formed on the clothing with painstaking care.
2. Be selective about the background.
When depicting a key scene, always incorporate special effects tone and draw a background. This will heighten the reader's interest.

3. Be selective about the composition.
Play around with composing from various perspectives when producing a psychological scene or a panel of the couple together. This will heighten the visual impact.
4. Be selective about etching.
Do not stop at adding tone. Be sure to etch the tone's edges with a brush as well. Both softly blurring the borders and creating clearly delineated etches will expand your range of portrayal.

Chapter 4

Manual

Chapter 1: Preliminaries

System Requirements
- Have installed at least one of the following:
  Adobe Photoshop 5.0/5.5/6.0/7.0/CS or Adobe Photoshop LE 5.0; Adobe Photoshop Elements 1.0/2.0; Jasc Paint Shop Pro 7.0/8.0.

- Use one of the following operating systems:
  Microsoft Windows 98 SE, Windows ME, Windows 2000, or Windows XP.

- Meet or exceed the following hardware specifications:
  Intel Pentium or 100% compatible CPU (Pentium 3 800 MHz or higher recommended)
  CD-ROM drive
  128MB RAM or more (256MB or more recommended)
  250MB or more of free local disk space (950MB or more recommended)

Adobe Photoshop Elements and Jasc Paint Shop Pro limit certain operations, and Computones' Autolayer functionality will not work with them. However, it is possible to manually create a new layer and lay it atop an image. For more details, consult the Software Functions Table on the next page. Further, there is no guarantee that this software will function perfectly with other Photoshop plug-in-compatible software packages that are not listed above.

1-2 Computones-Compatible Image File Formats
The image file formats Computones will and will not support are listed below.

Supported:
Grayscale
Duotone
RGB Color
CMYK Color
Lab Color

Not Supported:
Bitmap
Indexed Color
Multichannel
All 16 Bits/Channel modes

Chapter 2: Photoshop 5.0/5.5/6.0/7.0/CS

This chapter is for readers using Photoshop 5.0/5.5/6.0/7.0/CS.

Before You Install

These installation notes are for all supported operating systems (Microsoft Windows 98 SE, Windows Me, Windows 2000, or Windows XP).

• Make certain you have Photoshop 5.0, 5.5, 6.0, 7.0, or CS (hereafter "Photoshop") installed.

• Shut down any antivirus software or any other background applications, and adjust your operating system so that your machine does not go into sleep mode during installation.

• Having multiple graphics software packages installed on the same machine can interfere with the normal use of this software.

Installing Computones

"Computones" is made up of a tone plug-in and a Computones-specific data set made up of tones. Follow the installation steps below in order to use them.

Step 1

Insert the Computones CD-ROM into a CD-ROM drive.

Step 2

Double-click on the My Computer icon on the Windows desktop (Windows XP users should click on the Start Menu and then click on My Computer), and double-click on the Computones CD-ROM icon. The Computones Installer.exe (or simply "Computones Installer") icon will appear. Double-click on it to start the installation.

Step 3

You will be asked to which folder or directory you want to install Computones. Select "Install in the Photoshop Plug-Ins folder." The installer will then automatically search for the plug-ins folder and install Computones.

Step 4

Next, install the Computones-specific tone data set.

If "Also copy tone files" is checked, then the plug-in, tone data, and tone sets on the CD-ROM will be selected and written to the local disk.

If "Also copy tone files" is not checked, then Tone and other utility programs will be installed, but every time you use the plug-in, the tone data and sets on the CD-ROM will need to be read from it.

If "Browse for tone file install location" is checked together with "Also copy tone files," then you can choose to which folder you will install the tone files.

Step 5

When you click on the Install button, you will be prompted to confirm the install folder. If everything is OK, then click on the Yes button and the installation will begin. If there is a problem with the selected folder, then click on the No button. You will then have to check "Browse for tone file install location" and manually specify the install folder. When you have done so, click on the OK button.

- In the following cases, Computones will not be able to automatically search for an install folder, and so you must check "Browse for tone file install location" and then manually specify the install folder. This will also be necessary if the error message shown here should appear at any other point.

1) The Photoshop Plug-Ins folder has somehow been changed.
   The installer will only search for the Plug-Ins folder inside the Photoshop install folder. In any other case, manually specify the install location.

2) There is more than one graphics software package installation.
   The installer will automatically search for the Photoshop install folder. If the folder it finds is not what you normally use, then manually specify the install folder for you do normally use for Photoshop.

3) The automatic search may fail for reasons not covered by the above. In such cases, manually specify the Photoshop folder.

Step 6

When you have confirmed the install folder and hit the OK button, if you have checked "Also copy tone files," then a dialog box titled, "Select installation files" will appear. This box will not appear if you have not checked this option, and you may proceed to Step 8. The list on the left side of the window will show the tone file groups present on the CD-ROM, while the list on the right shows the tone file groups to be installed. If there is some tone file group in the list on the right that you will not be using, select it from the list and hit the Remove button. When all the file groups you want have been added, click on the OK button.

Step 7

If you have checked "Browse for tone file install location" and begun the installation, then you can choose where you wish to create the folder that will hold all the tone files. A dialog box will appear asking you about this; at that point, specify the folder as you wish. If you have not checked "Browse for tone file install location," then a tone file install folder will automatically be created within the plug-in install folder, and no dialog box will appear.

Step 8

Once the installation begins, a progress bar will be displayed. The installation may take some time, so if you are using a computer with a battery, please make sure you are also using an AC adapter when you install Computones. Hitting the Cancel button will stop the installation, and tone files in mid-installation will automatically be deleted. Once the installation is complete, a window will appear indicating so. Click on the OK button.

Step 9

After the installation is complete, launch Photoshop. If you select File → New... and create a new file, "Computones" will be displayed in the Filter menu. From there you can start using tones.

*If "Computones" is not displayed in the Filter menu, then it is possible that the folder in which the Plug-Ins reside and the plug-in install folder are different. You can check the location of the Plug-Ins folder at Edit → Preferences in Photoshop 6.0/7.0/CS (File → Preferences in Photoshop 5.0/5.5) under "Plug-Ins and Scratch Disks..."

Step 10

Once you have launched Photoshop, open the "Companion.psd" file located in the Sample folder on the Computones CD-ROM. Open the Filter menu and start up Computones. Immediately after startup, you will be asked just once for a serial number. Enter the serial number at the first of this book and click on OK.

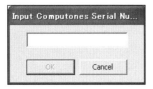

Step 11

Installation is now complete.

Try Using Some Tones
Let's get started right away!

Step 1

Start Photoshop, access Edit → Preferences in Photoshop 6.0/7.0 (Files → Preferences in Photoshop 5.0/5.5), and select "General..." A new window will open, and in that window is an Interpolation pull down menu. Select "Nearest Neighbor (fastest)" in that menu and click on OK.

Step 2

Select File → Open...and an Open window will appear so you can select a file to read in. Open the Companion.psd file in the Sample folder on the Computones CD-ROM.

Step 3

Adjust the resolution of the sample image you opened in Step 2. Adjust it to match the resolution of the printer you are using such that one is an integral multiple of the other. For example, if you are using a printer capable of printing 720 dpi images, set your image resolution to be 360 or 720 dpi. If the horizontal and vertical printer resolutions are different (for example, 1440 x 720 dpi), then your image resolution should be a multiple of one or the other. In theory, a 1440 dpi resolution would be usable, but from a quality perspective it is too high. A lower setting is better.

To change the image resolution in Photoshop, click on Image → Image Size... A window will pop up; input a new value where the "600" is displayed in the Resolution field. Keep in mind the units are in pixels/inch.

- If you don't know the output capabilities of your printer, it does not matter if you leave the setting (600 dpi) as is, but printed copies of your image may look blurry as a result.

Step 4

Use Photoshop's Magic Wand Tool to select the collar area of the clothing on the figure in your sample image. We will call this selected portion the "Tone Draw Area." Now set the Magic Wand Tool's Tolerance value to 1, and uncheck Anti-aliased.

- Please consult your Photoshop manual for more on the Magic Wand and its option bar. Using tones without specifying a Tone Draw Area will automatically make the entire image the effective Tone Draw Area.

Step 5

Select Filter → Computones → Tone...

- If "Computones" does not appear in the Filter menu, please go back to the "Installing Computones" section and review the installation process.

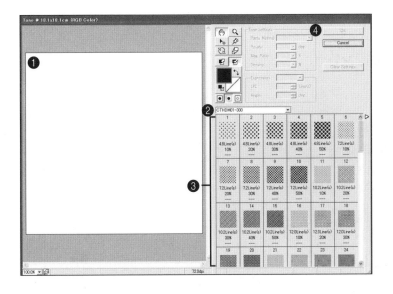

Step 6

In the middle of your screen, a Computones window will appear. At the left side of that window, there is a "Preview Display," and in it part of the image will be displayed at a 100% display ratio.❶

Step 7

Click on the Tone Set Selection pull-down menu and select the "CTHDM01-600" tone set. The contents of the tone set are displayed at the bottom right in the Tone Set Area.❷

- If you did not check the "Also copy tone files" box at installation, then every time you use tones they will be read directly from the Computones CD-ROM. Therefore, when you are using Computones you must make sure the CD-ROM is in the CD-ROM drive at all times.

Step 8

Try clicking on a tone you like from the Tone Set Area. We recommend you try out the "50.0 Line(s) 10%" dot tone. (If you don't see an exact match, choose a tone with similar values.)❸

Step 9

Click on a tone, and it will cover the Tone Draw Area you specified in Step 4. If you would like to change tones, just click on another tone in the Tone Set Area.

- If you'd like to specify a different Tone Draw Area, then you have to go back to Photoshop first, and execute this process from Step 4 again.

Step 10

If you would like to apply the effects you have created to the sample image, then hit the OK button. After the tone you have selected has been applied, you will go back to Photoshop. If you print out your work, you can see the real results in more minute detail.

If you would rather not apply the effects you have created to the sample image, then click on the Cancel button. The sample image will be unchanged, and you will return to Photoshop.❹

Chapter 3: Photoshop Elements 1.0/2.0

This chapter is for readers using Photoshop Elements 1.0/2.0.

Before You Install
These installation notes are for all supported operating systems (Microsoft Windows 98 SE, Windows Me, Windows 2000, or Windows XP).

- Make certain you have Photoshop Elements 1.0/2/0 (hereafter "Elements") installed.

- Shut down any antivirus software or any other background applications, and adjust your operating system so that your machine does not go into sleep mode during installation.

- Having multiple graphics software packages installed on the same machine can interfere with the normal use of this software.

Installing Computones
"Computones" is made up of a tone plug-in and a Computones-specific data set made up of tones. Follow the installation steps below in order to use them.

Step 1
Insert the Computones CD-ROM into a CD-ROM drive.

Step 2
Double-click on the My Computer icon on the Windows desktop (Windows XP users should click on the Start Menu and then click on My Computer), and double-click on the Computones CD-ROM icon. The Computones Installer.exe (or simply "Computones Installer") icon will appear. Double-click on it to start the installation.

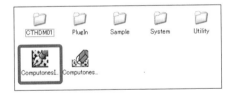

Step 3
You will be asked to which folder or directory you want to install Computones. Select "Install in the Photoshop Plug-Ins folder." The installer will then automatically search for the Photoshop Elements plug-ins folder and install Computones.

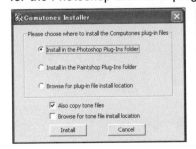 

Step 4

Next, install the Computones-specific tone data set.

If "Also copy tone files" is checked, then the plug-in, tone data, and tone sets on the CD-ROM will be selected and written to the local disk.

If "Also copy tone files" is not checked, then Tone and other utility programs will be installed, but every time you use the tone data and sets on the CD-ROM they will need to be read from it.

If "Browse for tone file install location" is checked together with "Also copy tone files," then you can choose to which folder you will install the tone files.

Step 5

When you click on the Install button, you will be prompted to confirm the install folder. If everything is OK, then click on the Yes button and the installation will begin. If there is a problem with the selected folder, then click on the No button. You will have to check "Browse for tone file install location" and then manually specify the install folder. When you have done so, click on the OK button.

- In the following cases, Computones will not be able to automatically search for an install folder, and so you must check "Browse for tone file install location" and then manually specify the install folder. This will also be necessary if any of the error messages shown here should appear at any other point.

1) The Photoshop Elements Plug-Ins folder has somehow been changed.
   The installer will only search for the Plug-Ins folder inside the Photoshop Elements install folder. In any other case, manually specify the install location.

2) There is more than one graphics software package installation.
   The installer will automatically search for the Photoshop Elements install folder. If the folder it finds is not what you normally use, then manually specify the install folder you do normally use for Photoshop Elements.

3) The automatic search may fail for reasons not covered by the above. In such cases, manually specify the Photoshop Elements folder.

Step 6

When you have confirmed the install folder and hit the OK button, if you have checked "Also copy tone files," then a dialog box titled, "Select installation files" will appear. This box will not appear if you have not checked this option, and you may proceed to Step 8. The list on the left side of the window will show the tone file groups present on the CD-ROM, while the list on the right shows the tone file groups to be installed. If there is some tone file group in the list on the right that you will not be using, select it from the list and hit the Remove button. When all the file groups you want have been added, click on the OK button.

Step 7

Ilf you have checked "Browse for tone file install location" and begun the installation, then you can choose where you wish to create the folder that will hold all the tone files. A dialog box will appear asking you about this; at that point, specify the folder as you wish. If you have not checked "Browse for tone file install location," then a tone file install folder will automatically be created within the plug-in install folder, and no dialog box will appear.

Step 8

Once the installation begins, a progress bar will be displayed. The installation may take some time, so if you are using a computer with a battery, please make sure you are also using an AC adapter when you install Computones. Hitting the Cancel button will stop the installation, and tone files in mid-installation will automatically be deleted. Once the installation is complete, a window will appear indicating so. Click on the OK button.

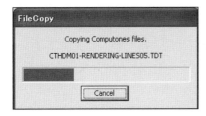

Step 9

After the installation is complete, launch Photoshop Elements. If you select File →
New... and create a new file, "Computones" will be displayed in the Filter menu. From
there you can start using tones.

If "Computones" is not displayed in the Filter menu, then it is possible that the folder
in which the Plug-Ins reside and the plug-in install folder are different. You can check
the location of the Plug-Ins folder at Edit → Preferences under "Plug-Ins and Scratch
Disks..."

Step 10

Once you have launched Photoshop Elements, open the "Companion.psd" file located
in the Sample folder on the Computones CD-ROM. Open the Filter menu and start up
Computones. Immediately after startup, you will be asked just once for a serial
number. Enter the serial number at the first of this book and click on OK.

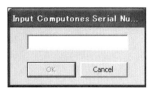

Step 11

Installation is now complete.

Try Using Some Tones
Let's get started right away!

Step 1
Start Photoshop Elements, select File → Open... and an Open window will appear so you can select a file to read in. Open the Companion.psd file in the Sample folder on the Computones CD-ROM.

- If you are unsure how to use File → Open..., please consult the Photoshop Elements manual.

Step 2
Adjust the resolution of the sample image you opened in Step 1. Adjust it to match the resolution of the printer you are using such that one is an integral multiple of the other. For example, if you are using a printer capable of printing 720 dpi images, set your image resolution to be 360 or 720 dpi. If the horizontal and vertical printer resolutions are different (for example, 1440 x 720 dpi), then your image resolution should be a multiple of one or the other. In theory, a 1440 dpi resolution would be usable, but from a quality perspective it is too high. A lower setting is better.

To change the image resolution in Photoshop Elements, click on Image → Image Size... A window will pop up; input a new value where the "600" is displayed in the Resolution field. Keep in mind the units are in pixels/inch, and in the lower part of the same window, "Resample Image" is set to "Nearest Neighbor."

- If you don't know the output capabilities of your printer, it does not matter if you leave the setting (600 dpi) as is, but printed copies of your image may look blurry as a result.

Step 3
Use Photoshop Elements' Magic Wand Tool to select the collar area of the clothing on the figure in your sample image. We will call this selected portion the "Tone Draw Area." Now set the Magic Wand Tool's Tolerance value to 1, and uncheck Anti-aliased.

- Please consult your Photoshop Elements manual for more on the Magic Wand and its option bar. Using tones without specifying a Tone Draw Area will automatically make the entire image the effective Tone Draw Area.

Step 4
Select Filter → Computones → Tone...

*If "Computones" does not appear in the Filter menu, please go back to the "Installing Computones" section and review the installation process.

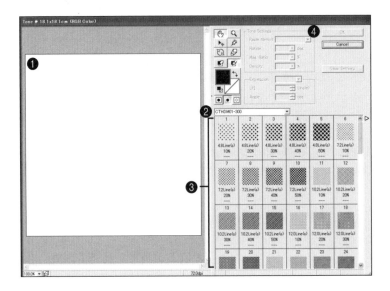

Step 5
In the middle of your screen, a Computones window will appear. At the left side of that window, there is a "Preview Display," and in it part of the image will be displayed at a 100% display ratio.❶

Step 6
Click on the Tone Set Selection pull-down menu and select the "CTHDM01-600" tone set. The contents of the tone set are displayed at the bottom right in the Tone Set Area.❷

*If you did not check the "Also copy tone files" box at installation, then every time you use tones they will be read directly from the Computones CD-ROM. Therefore, when you are using Computones you must make sure the CD-ROM is in the CD-ROM drive at all times.

Step 7
Try clicking on a tone you like from the Tone Set Area. We recommend you try out the "55.0 Line(s) 40%" dot tone. (If you don't see an exact match, choose a tone with similar values.)❸

Step 8

Click on a tone, and it will cover the Tone Draw Area you specified in Step 3. If you would like to change tones, just click on another tone in the Tone Set Area.

• If you'd like to specify a different Tone Draw Area, then you have to go back to Photoshop Elements first, and execute this process from Step 3 again.

Step 9

If you would like to apply the effects you have created to the sample image, then hit the OK button. After the tone you have selected has been applied, you will go back to Photoshop Elements. If you print out your work, you can see the real results in more minute detail.❹

If you would rather not apply the effects you have created to the sample image, then click on the Cancel button. The sample image will be unchanged, and you will return to Photoshop Elements.

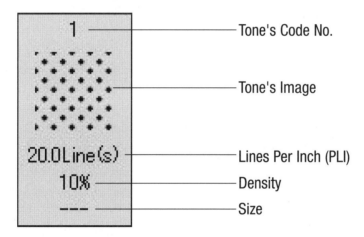

Tone's Code No.

Tone's Image

Lines Per Inch (PLI)

Density

Size

Chapter 4: Jasc Paint Shop Pro 7.0/8.0

This chapter is for readers using Jasc Paint Shop Pro 7.0/8.0.

Before You Install

These installation notes are for all supported operating systems (Microsoft Windows 98 SE, Windows Me, Windows 2000, or Windows XP).

• Make certain you have Jasc Paint Shop Pro 7.0/8.0 (hereafter "Paint Shop Pro") installed.

• Shut down any antivirus software or any other background applications, and adjust your operating system so that your machine does not go into sleep mode during installation.

• Having multiple graphics software packages installed on the same machine can interfere with the normal use of this software.

Installing Computones

"Computones" is made up of a tone plug-in and a Computones-specific data set made up of tones. Follow the installation steps below in order to use them.

Step 1
Insert the Computones CD-ROM into a CD-ROM drive.

Step 2
Double-click on the My Computer icon on the Windows desktop (Windows XP users should click on the Start Menu and then click on My Computer), and double-click on the Computones CD-ROM icon. The Computones Installer.exe (or simply "Computones Installer") icon will appear. Double-click on it to start the installation.

Step 3
You will be asked to which folder or directory you want to install Computones. Select "Install in the Paint Shop Pro Plug-Ins folder." The installer will then automatically search for the Paint Shop Pro plug-ins folder and install Computones.

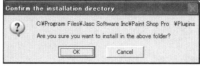

Step 4

Next, install the Computones-specific tone data set.

If "Also copy tone files" is checked, then the plug-in, tone data, and tone sets on the CD-ROM will be selected and written to the local disk.

If "Also copy tone files" is not checked, then Tone and other utility programs will be installed, but every time you use the plug-in, the tone data and sets on the CD-ROM will need to be read from it.

If "Browse for tone file install location" is checked together with "Also copy tone files," then you can choose to which folder you will install the tone files.

Step 5

When you click on Install, the installer will ask you to select the folder designated for Paint Shop Pro Plug-Ins if there are multiple folders present. If there is only one folder designated as such, then hit the OK button and the installation will begin. If there is some kind of problem with the install folder, then you will have to hit the No button, check the "Browse for tone file install location" box, and specify the folder manually. When you are done, hit the OK button.

Step 6

When you have confirmed the install folder and hit the OK button, if you have checked "Also copy tone files," then a dialog box titled, "Select installation files" will appear. This box will not appear if you have not checked this option, and you may proceed to Step 8. The list on the left side of the window will show the tone file groups present on the CD-ROM, while the list on the right shows the tone file groups to be installed. If there is some tone file group in the list on the right that you will not be using, select it from the list and hit the Remove button. When all the file groups you want have been added, click on the OK button.

Step 7

IIf you have checked "Browse for tone file install location" and begun the installation, then you can choose where you wish to create the folder that will hold all the tone files. A dialog box will appear asking you about this; at that point, specify the folder as you wish. If you have not checked "Browse for tone file install location," then a tone file install folder will automatically be created within the plug-in install folder, and no dialog box will appear.

Step 8

Once the installation begins, a progress bar will be displayed. The installation may take some time, so if you are using a computer with a battery, please make sure you are also using an AC adapter when you install Computones. Hitting the Cancel button will stop the installation, and tone files in mid-installation will automatically be deleted. Once the installation is complete, a window will appear indicating so. Click on the OK button.

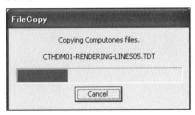

Step 9

After the installation is complete, launch Paint Shop Pro. If you select File → New... and create a new file, "Computones" will be displayed in the Filter menu. From there you can start using tones.

If "Computones" is not displayed in the Filter menu, then it is possible that the folder in which the Plug-Ins reside and the plug-in install folder are different. You can check the location of the Plug-Ins folder at Edit → Preferences under "Plug-Ins and Scratch Disks..."

Step 10

Once you have launched Paint Shop Pro, open the "Companion.psd" file located in the Sample folder on the Computones CD-ROM. Open the Filter menu and start up Computones. Immediately after startup, you will be asked just once for a serial number. Enter the serial number at the first of this book and click on OK.

Try Using Some Tones
Let's get started right away!

Step 1
Start Paint Shop Pro, select File → Open... and an Open window will appear so you can select a file to read in. Open the Companion.psd file in the Sample folder on the Computones CD-ROM.

- If you are unsure how to use File → Open..., please consult the Paint Shop Pro manual.

Step 2
Adjust the resolution of the sample image you opened in Step 1. Adjust it to match the resolution of the printer you are using such that one is an integral multiple of the other. For example, if you are using a printer capable of printing 720 dpi images, set your image resolution to be 360 or 720 dpi. If the horizontal and vertical printer resolutions are different (for example, 1440 x 720 dpi), then your image resolution should be a multiple of one or the other. In theory, a 1440 dpi resolution would be usable, but from a quality perspective it is too high. A lower setting is better.

To change the image resolution in Paint Shop Pro, click on Image → Resize... A window will pop up; check "Actual/print size" and input a new value where the "600.000" is displayed in the Resolution field. Keep in mind the units are in pixels/inch, and in the lower part of the same window, "Resize type" is set to "Pixel Resize."

- If you don't know the output capabilities of your printer, it does not matter if you leave the setting (600 dpi) as is, but printed copies of your image may look blurry as a result.

Step 3
After you click on the Magic Wand in the Tool palette, set the options in the Tool Options palette as follows:

1) Set the Match Mode to "RGB Value."
2) Set the Tolerance to 1.
3) Set Feather to 0.

- Please consult your Paint Shop Pro manual for more on the Magic Wand and its Tool Option palette.

Step 4

Use Photoshop Elements' Magic Wand Tool to select the collar area of the clothes on the figure in your sample image. We will call this selected portion the "Tone Draw Area."

*Using tones without specifying a Tone Draw Area will automatically make the entire image the effective Tone Draw Area.

Step 5

Select Effects → Plugin Filter → Computones → Tone...

*If "Computones" does not appear in the Plugin Filter menu, please go back to the "Installing Computones" section and review the installation process.

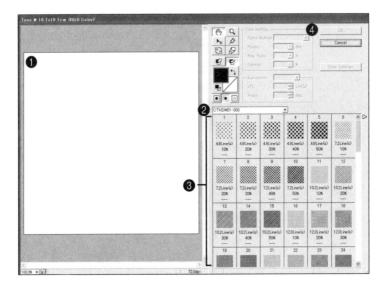

Step 6

In the middle of your screen, a Computones window will appear. At the left side of that window, there is a "Preview Display," and in it part of the image will be displayed at a 100% display ratio.❶

Step 7

Click on the Tone Set Selection pull-down menu and select the "CTHDM01-600" tone set. The contents of the tone set are displayed at the bottom right in the Tone Set Area.❷

*If you did not check the "Also copy tone files" box at installation, then every time you use tones they will be read directly from the Computones CD-ROM. Therefore, when you are using Computones you must make sure the CD-ROM is in the CD-ROM drive at all times.

Step 8

Try clicking on a tone you like from the Tone Set Area. We recommend you try out the "55.0 Line(s) 40%" dot tone. ❸

Step 9

Click on a tone, and it will cover the Tone Draw Area you specified in Step 4. If you would like to change tones, just click on another tone in the Tone Set Area.

- If you'd like to specify a different Tone Draw Area, then you have to go back to Paint Shop Pro first, and execute this process from Step 4 again.

Step 10

If you would like to apply the effects you have created to the sample image, then hit the OK button. After the tone you have selected has been applied, you will go back to Paint Shop Pro. If you print out your work, you can see the real results in more minute detail. ❹

If you would rather not apply the effects you have created to the sample image, then click on the Cancel button. The sample image will be unchanged, and you will return to Paint Shop Pro.

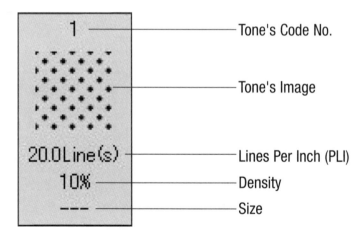

Tone's Code No.

Tone's Image

Lines Per Inch (PLI)

Density

Size

Uninstallation

Follow the steps below to uninstall Computones and completely remove it from your local disk.

Step 1
Insert the Computones CD-ROM into a CD-ROM drive.

Step 2
Double-click on the My Computer icon on the Windows desktop (Windows XP users should click on the Start Menu and then click on My Computer), and double-click on the Computones CD-ROM icon. The Computones Uninstaller.exe (or simply "Computones Uninstaller") icon will appear. Double-click on it to start the uninstallation.

Step 3
Next, a dialog box will appear. Choose an uninstallation method and hit the OK button.

"Remove only the plug-in folder"
This option removes the Computones plug-in itself only. The installed tone files stay as they are.

"Remove only the tone folders"
This option completely removes all the installed tone files. The plug-in file will remain, so the Computones plug-in will still be usable.

"Remove both the plug-in and tone folders"
This option completely removes all the installed plug-in and tone files.

Step 4
After starting the uninstaller, all the data covered by the option selected in Step 3 will be removed.

• If you install Computones more than once without uninstalling it, then only the most recently installed plug-in and/or tone files will be removed.

Step 5
If the uninstallation process completes normally, a message indicating so will appear. Hit the OK button.

• If the Computones installer was not used to install Computones, then an error message will appear. The same error will occur if you attempt to remove the tone folder when it does not exist on the local disk. In order to use the uninstaller, the Computones installer must have been used in the first place.

Chapter 5: Computones Functionality Overview

Tone Functions

The area selected via your graphic software determines the area in an image where a tone will be applied. If no such selection is made, then the tone will be applied to the entire image. For normal use, it is recommended that you first use your graphic software to select where in the image the tone is to be applied.

If your screen appears pink, it means that part of your image has been specified as a tone draw area. The actual draw area is the portion not shown in pink, but in white or gray.

1) Preview Display

You can use this display to see how your image would look with a tone applied. You can use the scroll bars at the right and bottom of the display to scroll through the preview.

2) Selected Tone Info Area

The name, lines per inch (LPI), density, size, and other information on the tone currently applied to the Tone Draw Area are shown here. However, if the tone window is narrow, then all the information might not be displayed. Widening the window will reveal everything.

3) Preview Display Mode button

By turning this button on or off, you can display only the selected area ("Off") or you can display all possible layers, one on top of the other ("On").

• This function is not available in Paint Shop Pro.

4) Preview Display Ratio

Much like the Zoom Tool, clicking on this pull-down menu and then choosing one of the 13 choices inside it changes the display ratio of the image in the preview display. The choices are spread over 13 different steps between 5% and 800%, so you can zoom in or out on your image.

5) Image Resolution

This constant display shows the resolution of your image in dots per inch (DPI).

6) Hand Tool button

Clicking this button will start the Hand Tool, and the cursor will take the shape of a hand. You can use the hand tool to move the image around in the preview display. You can do the same thing with the scroll bars; however, they cannot move pins or applied tones separately.

7) Move Tool button

Hitting this button brings up the Move Tool, and the cursor will change into an arrowhead with four-way arrow. Using it in the preview display allows you to move a pin or an applied tone without moving the image itself.

8) Rotate Tool button

Clicking this button starts the Rotate Tool, and the cursor will change into a curly double arrow. Clicking and dragging on an image with this tool will rotate an applied tone around a pin.

9) Zoom Tool button

Hitting this button brings up the Zoom Tool, and turns your cursor into magnifying glass. You can use this tool to zoom in or out on the preview display over 13 steps, from 5% to 800%. Clicking on the preview display with the Zoom Tool icon as is will zoom in, while holding down the Alt key and clicking on it will zoom out.

10) Pin Tool button

Clicking on this button starts the Pin Tool, turning the cursor into a pin. The Pin Tool "pins" a tone down to a location of your choosing, and then serves as an axis around which you can rotate a tone. You can move the pin by clicking on the preview display; its default location is in the upper right corner of the image.

11) Scale Tool button

Hit this button to bring up the Scale Tool, and the cursor will turn into a double-ended arrow. You can then change the dimensions of an applied tone in all directions (centered on a pin) while maintaining the same image aspect ratio. Also, the magnification factor is indicated in a separate field; you can change this factor by directly entering a different value.

12) Use Host Color button

Hitting this button sets the foreground color to whatever color you are using in Photoshop or another host application, and renders the background transparent. If your Image Mode is set to Render Foreground and Background Colors, then the foreground color is set to transparent, and the background color will be set to whatever color you are using in your host application.

13) Use Custom Color button

If your Image Mode is set to Render Foreground and Background Colors when you press this button, then the foreground color will be rendered in 100% black, and the background color will be set to 100% white. If the Image Mode is set to Render in Foreground Color, then the foreground color will be set to transparent, and the background to 100% white.

14) Foreground Color Selection box

Clicking on this box will start up the Color Picker, and you can use it to change the foreground color. By doing so, you can also change the color of the tone you will be applying. The default foreground color is 100% black. If your Image Mode is set to Render in Foreground Color, the default is set to transparent.

• If you are unfamiliar with the usage of the Color Picker, please refer to your graphic software manual.

15) Restore Default Foreground and Background Colors icon

Clicking this icon sets the foreground color to 100% black and the background color to transparent. If you set the foreground or background colors to anything except 100% black, 100% white, or transparent, this icon will turn into a caution symbol.

16) Swap Foreground and Background Colors icon

Clicking this icon switches the foreground and background colors. You can produce black and white inversion effects this way.

17) Set Background Color box

Clicking on this box will open the Color Picker, and you can use it to change the background color. The default background color is transparent, but if your Image Mode is set to Render Foreground and Background Colors or Render in Background Color, the default is set to 100% white.

- If you are unfamiliar with the usage of the Color Picker, please refer to your graphic software manual.

18) Render Foreground and Background Colors button

Hitting this button will set the Image Mode to "Render Foreground and Background Colors." In Render Foreground and Background Colors mode, it is possible to color both the foreground and background. Each time you start using Tone, the foreground and background color settings will be as you left them the previous time.

19) Render in Background Color button

Hitting this button sets the Image Mode to Render in Background Color. In this mode the background color is set to transparent.

20) Render in Foreground Color button

Hitting this button sets the Image Mode to Render in Foreground Color. In this mode the foreground color appears transparent and is not visible.

21) Paste Method selection

You can choose how you apply a tone by choosing among the selections in this pull-down menu. For dot, line, and sand duotones, you can choose repeat or flip repeat. For radiating line and pattern duotones and grayscales, you can choose flip, flip repeat, don't repeat, no-flip repeat, and fold over.

22) Rotate field

Input a value in this field to rotate a tone as you wish. You can input any value from -360 degrees to 360 degrees in increments of 0.1 degrees. Inputting a value greater than 360 will result in the difference between that value and 360 being input. To enter the value after you input it, hit the Enter key or click anywhere on the tone. Hitting the Enter key twice will close the Tone window, so be careful.

23) Rotate Slide

You can also set a rotation angle by dragging the Angle Slide. The slide can move from -358 degrees to 358 degrees, in two-degree increments. The center, extreme left, and extreme right of the slide bar are set to zero degrees.

24) Magnification Ratio field

Entering a value in this field sets the magnification factor of your display. You can enter any value from 10% to 1000% in increments of 0.1%. To enter the value after you input it, hit the Enter key or click anywhere on the tone. Hitting the Enter key twice will close the Tone window, so be careful.

25) Magnification Ratio Slide

You can also set a magnification ratio by dragging the Magnification Ratio Slide. The slide can move from 10% magnification to 1000%, in 0.1% increments. The center of the slide bar is set to 100%. If you have specified a Tone Draw Area, then when you drag this slide the area will turn either white or gray, and the rest of the image will turn pink. To close the Magnification Ratio Slide, click anywhere outside the slide.

26) Density field

This field is only for grayscale tones. Entering a value in this field sets the density of a tone. You can enter any value from 20% to 180% in increments of 0.1%. To enter the value after you input it, hit the Enter key or click anywhere on the tone. Hitting the Enter key twice will close the Tone window, so be careful.

27) Density Slide

This field is only for grayscale tones. You can also set the density by dragging the Density Slide. The slide can move from 20% density to 180%, in 0.5% increments. The center of the slide bar is set to 100%. To close the Density Slide, click anywhere outside the slide.

28) Expression field

This field is only for grayscale tones. The choices of expression are None, Dots, Line, Cross, and Random. Choosing "None" will apply no dot shading.

29) LPI field

This field is only for grayscale tones; enter a lines per inch (LPI) value here as you like to apply dot shading. You can enter values from 1 to 85 in 0.1 increments. To enter the value after you input it, hit the Enter key or click anywhere on the tone. Hitting the Enter key twice will close the Tone window, so be careful. If you want to avoid "tone jumping," then you should specify 20 LPI for an image at 300 dpi or less, and 40 LPI for an image at 600 dpi or less.

- You must have something other than "none" selected in the Expression field in order to use this.

30) LPI Input button

This field is only for grayscale tones. You can specify the LPI value for applying dot shading to your selected grayscale tone at an angle of your choosing. Each click of the button steps through from 20 LPI to 27.5, 32.5, 42.5, 50, 55, 60, 65, 70, 75, to 80 LPI, displaying your image appropriately at each step. If you want to avoid "tone jumping," then you should specify 20 LPI for an image at 300 dpi or less, and 40 LPI for an image at 600 dpi or less.

- You must have something other than "none" selected in the Expression field in order to use this.

31) Angle field

This one is for grayscale tones only. You can specify the LPI value for applying dot shading to your selected grayscale tone at an angle of your choosing. You can input any value from -360 degrees to 360 degrees in increments of 0.1 degrees. We recommend that you normally use a 45-degree setting. To enter the value after you input it, hit the Enter key or click anywhere on the tone. Hitting the Enter key twice will close the Tone window, so be careful.

- You must have something other than "none" selected in the Expression field in order to use this one.

32) Angle adjustment buttons

These buttons are for grayscale tones only. By manipulating the upper and lower buttons, you can specify an angle as you like to apply dot shading. Each click of the button steps through from 0 degrees to 15, 30, 45, 60, 75, 90, 105, 120, 135, 150, and 165 degrees, displaying your image appropriately at each step. You will not be able to set this angle if you have "random" selected in the Expression field.

- You must have something other than "none" selected in the Expression field in order to use this one.

33) OK button

Hitting this button will set the tone and any modifications you have made onto your image, and return you to your graphic application. The parameters you set while using Tone will be remembered, and the next time you start it up they will be as you left them.

34) Cancel button

Hitting this button will cancel setting the tone and any modifications you have made onto your image, and return you to your graphic application. The parameters you set while using Tone will be remembered, and the next time you start it up they will be as you left them.

35) Clear Settings button

Pushing this button will reset any values you have changed to their defaults, which are as follows.
- Paste Method: Repeat, Angle: 0 degrees, Magnification: 100%, Density: 100%, Expression: Dot, LPI: 60, Angle: 45 degrees.

36) Tone Set Selection pull-down menu

This changes the tone set you wish to use. Click on this menu and select a tone set from those displayed. Then, by moving on to choose a tone set from among those in the tone set display, you can display its contents on your screen. A maximum of 20 sets within a single tone set can be displayed

- There may not be any tone set selections displayed in this field. In that case, proceed as follows:

  1. Create a new tone set by hitting the Menu button and using the "New Tone Set..." command.
  2. Import a tone set by hitting the Menu button, selecting Import Tone Set File, and saving a tone set as you wish..

37) Tone Information Display

When you select a tone from within the tone set display, a variety of information about that tone is displayed. In the Tone Information Display, from left to right, you will find the tone set index number, title, LPI, density, and size of the tone. Further, a "---" is displayed where no information is available or there is no need to display anything.

*About the tone information headings
The tone set index number is a number attached to every tone and displayed next to it in the tone set display. The numbers run from the top left tone across to the right and down, counting off each tone.

The title indicates some characteristic of a tone.

The LPI value shows how many lines of dots per inch make up a tone. For the most part, other than dot and line screens, most tones do not have this information, so nothing is displayed. Sand tones have an LPI value, but this is approximate.

Density is expressed as a percentage for each tone. A perfectly white tone has a 0% density, while a perfectly black one has 100%. A display of "100-0%" or "100-0-100%" means a given tone is a gradation.

Size is the length by width dimensions of a tone in centimeters. Tones with only a single value displayed are pattern tones with no boundary on either their width or length.

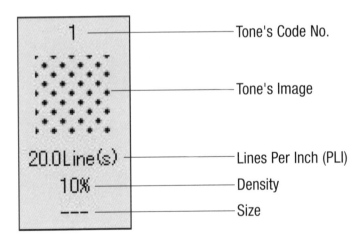

1 ——————————— Tone's Code No.

——————————— Tone's Image

20.0Line(s) ——————————— Lines Per Inch (PLI)

10% ——————————— Density

--- ——————————— Size

38) Menu button
Pressing this button brings up the Menu.

Supplement: Tone Set Registration and Building
If you did not check the "Also copy tone files" box at installation, the necessary tone files will not be on your local disk, meaning you cannot automatically register a tone set. The steps for manually registering and building a tone set are shown below.

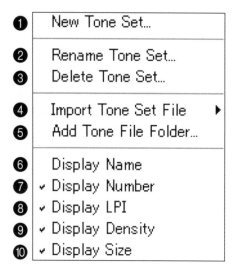

❶ New Tone Set...
This command creates a new tone set on your local disk. You can use this command by selecting it from the tone set selection field, and you can create up to 1000 tone sets. When you use this command, a dialog box will appear, asking you to name your tone set. Once you've given it a name you like, click on OK to create a tone set. Click on the Cancel button to cancel the command.

❷ Rename Tone Set...
This command changes the name of the current tone set. Using it makes a dialog box appear asking you for a new tone set name. After you have entered a name you like, click on the OK button and the name will be changed. If you want to cancel the name change, hit the Cancel button.

❸ Delete Tone Set...

This command deletes the current tone set. However, the tones themselves will not be deleted and will remain on your local disk. Using this command will bring up a confirmation dialog box. If you wish to delete the tone set, click on Yes. If you do not, click on No.

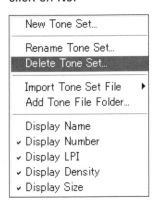 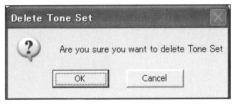

❹ Import Tone Set File

This command imports a new tone set you would like to use and adds it behind the current tone set. Using this command brings up a submenu — click on View File. Another dialog box will appear to ask you where the next tone set you would like to import is located. Click on a tone set file (extension ".tst") and click on Open. If you want to cancel the import, click on Cancel. If you click on the list of previously added tone set files, you can choose a set from there as well.

- If you do not want to put the tone set you wish to import inside the tone set you are currently using, first use the Create New Tone Set command from the Menu to create a new set, and then import your desired tone set file to there.

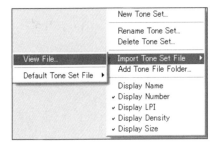

❺ Add Tone File Folder...

Use this command to add all the tones in a folder you specify to the end of the current tone set in one stroke. Executing this command brings up a dialog box asking you for the location of the tone file folder. Choose the folder you wish and click on the OK button. If you wish to cancel the command, click on Cancel. Folders located inside the folder you specify can also be searched.

- **Add Tone File...**
  This command adds a single tone file to the end of the current tone set. Using this

command brings up a dialog box asking you for the location of the tone file you wish to add. Choose the ".tdt" file you wish and click on Open. If you wish to cancel the command, click on Cancel.

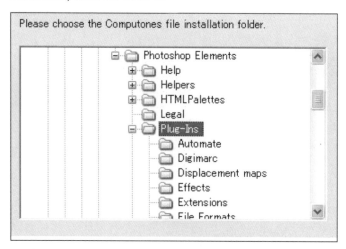

❻ Display Name
Using this command switches between displaying all tone names and displaying all tone thumbnails.

❼ Display Number
Using this command switches the display of all visible tone numbers on and off.

❽ Display LPI
Using this command switches the display of all visible tone LPI values on and off.

❾ Display Density
Using this command switches the display of all visible tone density values on and off.

❿ Display Size
Using this command switches the display of all visible tone sizes on and off.

Tone Set Display

This command displays the contents of the selected tone set at a glance. A total of 1200 tones, 6 across and 200 down, can be displayed at once. You can execute the following actions on a single tone therein:

Click: The selected tone is applied to the Tone Draw Area.
Double Click: Same effect as hitting the OK button after the selected tone is applied.
Ctrl + Drag: Moves the selected tone as you wish.
Selecting a Tone: Displays the tone's information in the tone information display area. This area will appear blank if the display area is not open.
Right Click: Opens up an embedded smaller menu with the following commands.

Add Tone File...

This command inserts a tone directly before the selected one. Using this command brings up a dialog box asking you for the location of the tone file you wish to add. Choose the ".tdt" file you wish and click on Open. If you wish to cancel the command, click on Cancel. Using this command to add a tone will shift all the following tone files' numbers, so care must be taken when importing tone palette files and the like.

Add White Space

This command inserts or adds a blank space after the selected tone set. Clicking on a blank allows you to reset the currently applied tone.

Select All

This command selects all of the tones loaded into the tone display area.

Insert White Space

This command inserts or adds a blank space directly in front of the selected tone. Clicking on a blank allows you to reset the currently applied tone. Using this command to add a tone will shift all the following tone files' numbers, so care must therefore be taken when importing tone palette files and the like.

Remove

Using this command removes only the selected tone from the tone set. The tone itself is not deleted from your local disk.

File Info...

Using this command displays a tone's full path in a new window. Click on OK to close it.

Using Shortcut Keys

Shortcut key combinations are available for the commands listed below.

Tone Shortcuts:
Spacebar → Hand Tool
Alt → Zoom Out
Ctrl → Zoom In
Alt + Spacebar → Rotate
Ctrl + Spacebar → Scale
Alt + Ctrl → Move
Alt + Ctrl + Space → Pin

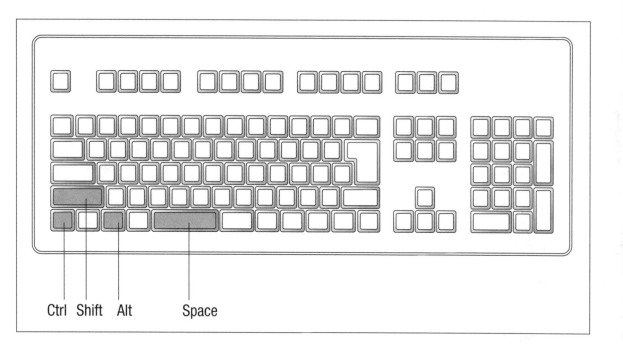

Ctrl   Shift   Alt   Space

Error Message Overview

The various Computones error messages are listed below. Should any others occur, as they are related to your operating system and/or graphic software, please consult the appropriate manual for a solution.

Error: Insufficient memory.
Cause: The PC does not have enough memory to run Computones
Solution: Shut down any other open applications or clear the internal memory in use by another graphic application to free up system memory and reserve it. (For more details, please see your graphic software manual.) If after this you still do not have enough memory, then you must increase the amount of physical system memory. The more internal system memory you have, the smoother Computones will operate.

Error: Incorrect serial number.
Cause: The serial number has not been input correctly.
Solution: You will only be asked once for the serial number. Check the number at the end of this book, make sure you have entered it correctly, and click on the OK button.

Error: Not a tone file.
Cause: You have specified a non-tone file for import.
Solution: Select a Computones-compatible tone file (.tdt).

Error: Not a tone set file.
Cause: You have specified a non-tone set file for import.
Solution: Select a Computones-compatible tone set file (.tst).

Error: Too many items. Cannot add to the tone set.
Cause: You are trying to add over 1002 tones to a single tone set.
Solution: A single tone set can hold a maximum of 1002 tones. To set or add more tones, use Menu → Create New Tone Set...

Error: An error has occurred.

Cause: Something other than the above has caused an error.

Solution: Make sure you are using a Computones-compatible environment. Reboot your computer and attempt to continue. If the same error appears, try reserving system memory. If problems still persist, then uninstall Computones and try reinstalling it. If even after that you still get the same error, then there is probably some issue with your operating system.

Error: An "X" is displayed in place of a tone file in a tone set, as shown in figure 1.

Cause: A tone file that is specified within the tone set cannot be found. The file itself is not present, and only the file path has been retained. If the CD-ROM drive or the local disk label has changed, or if there has been some other change in the computing environment, then this problem can occur.

Solution: Take the following steps. Select the tone in question, and then click on the following, in order: Menu → Delete Tone Set... → Yes → Create New Tone Set... → Input new tone set name → Import Tone Set File... → Browse Files... → Choose a tone set file → Open.

When the tone set is displayed as in figure 2 at the right, then the process is complete.

Question & Answer

Q How do I install Computones for Photoshop Elements 2?

A To install Computones for Adobe Photoshop Elements 2.0, follow the steps shown below.

1. Insert the Computones CD-ROM into a CD-ROM or DVD-ROM drive.

2. Double-click on the My Computer icon on the Windows desktop (Windows XP users should click on the Start Menu and then click on My Computer), and double-click on the Computones CD-ROM icon → Computones Installer.exe (or simply "Computones Installer").

3. You will be asked to which folder or directory you want to install Computones. Check the "Browse for plug-in file install location" radio button.

4. Choose a tone file install method, and click Install. A "Browse for Folder" dialog box will appear, allowing you to select the plug-in file install location. Click on the Local Disk (C:) → Program Files → Adobe → Photoshop Elements 2 → Plug-Ins. When you have selected the folder, click OK. If you have installed Photoshop Elements 2 to some other location, then select the Plug-Ins folder accordingly.

5. A "Confirm the installation directory" dialog box will appear. Check the file install location and click Yes to continue. If there is something wrong with the location, click No and repeat this process from step 3.

6. If you have checked the "Also copy tone files" box, then a "Browse for Folder" dialog box will appear. Add or remove tone files as you see fit, and click OK.

Once all installations are complete, an "Installation complete" dialog will appear. If the installation failed, repeat this process from step 2.

Q I cannot select any files to install, so I cannot install Computones!

A If during the Computones installation, the "Select installation files" dialog box has nothing displayed in the "Files to be installed" and "Files on the CD" lists, and you cannot continue with the installation, follow the steps shown below.

1. Insert the Computones CD-ROM into a CD-ROM or DVD-ROM drive.

2. Double-click on the My Computer icon on the Windows desktop (Windows XP users should click on the Start Menu and then click on My Computer), and double-click on the Computones CD-ROM icon → Computones Installer.exe (or simply "Computones Installer").

3. You will be asked to which folder or directory you want to install Computones. Check whichever radio button you like, uncheck "Also copy tone files," and click the Install button.

4. A "Confirm the installation directory" dialog box will appear. Check the file install location and click Yes to continue. If there is something wrong with the location, click No and repeat this process from step 3.

At this point the Computones plug-in and utility file installation is complete.

5. Next, install the tone files. Open up the Computones folder at its install location, create a new folder, and rename it "ToneFolder." You can verify the folder's install location in step 4 via the "Confirm the installation directory" dialog box.

6. Select the CTHDM01 folder on the Computones CD-ROM and choose one of the following methods to copy it to the Computones folder on your local disk.

   ➊ Right click on the CTHDM01 folder, and click on Copy from the pop up menu. Then right click on any blank space inside the Computones folder on your local disk and choose Paste.
   ➋ Drag the tone folders from the CD-ROM and drop them on some empty space inside Computones folder on your local disk.

7. The tone file installation is now complete. Next, start up Tones, click the Menu button, select Import Tone Set File → View File..., and import the tone file sets you just installed. If you copied tone set files that you do not need, use one of the methods below to remove them.

   ➊ If there are tones at certain resolutions you do not need, then put the entire 300 dpi or 600 dpi folders in the Recycle Bin to remove them.
   ➋ If there are certain tone genres you do not need, then open each resolution folder and place the Dot, Hatching, etc. folders in the Recycle Bin to remove them. Also remove tone set files like PT3-600-ALL.tst. that contain tones of all genres.

Q A "Cannot find the tone folder" message appears, and I cannot install Computones!

A If during the Computones installation, a "Cannot find the tone folder" message appears, and you cannot continue with the installation, follow the steps shown below.

1. Insert the Computones CD-ROM into a CD-ROM or DVD-ROM drive.

2. Double-click on the My Computer icon on the Windows desktop (Windows XP users should click on the Start Menu and then click on My Computer), and double-click on the Computones CD-ROM icon → Computones Installer.exe (or simply "Computones Installer").

Question & Answer

3. You will be asked to which folder or directory you want to install Computones. Check whichever radio button you like, uncheck "Also copy tone files," and click the Install button.

4. A "Confirm the installation directory" dialog box will appear. Check the file install location and click Yes to continue. If there is something wrong with the location, click No and repeat this process from step 3.

At this point the Computones plug-in and utility file installation is complete.

5. Next, install the tone files. Open up the Computones folder at its install location, create a new folder, and rename it "ToneFolder." You can verify the folder's install location in step 4 via the "Confirm the installation directory" dialog box.

6. Select the CTHDM01 folder on the Computones CD-ROM and choose one of the following methods to copy it to the Computones folder on your local disk.

   ❶ Right click on the CTHDM01 folder, and click on Copy from the pop up menu. Then right click on any blank space inside the Computones folder on your local disk and choose Paste.
   ❷ Drag the tone folders from the CD-ROM and drop them on some empty space inside Computones folder on your local disk.

7. The tone file installation is now complete. Next, start up Tones, click the Menu button, select Import Tone Set File → View File..., and import the tone file sets you just installed. If you copied tone set files that you do not need, use one of the methods below to remove them.

   ❶ If there are tones at certain resolutions you do not need, then put the entire 300 dpi or 600 dpi folders in the Recycle Bin to remove them.
   ❷ If there are certain tone genres you do not need, then open each resolution folder and place the Dot, Hatching, etc. folders in the Recycle Bin to remove them.

Q A "Computones may not have been installed" message appears, and I cannot install Computones!

A If during the Computones installation, a "The main Computones application may not have been installed" message appears, and you cannot continue with the installation, follow the steps shown below.

1. Insert the Computones CD-ROM into a CD-ROM or DVD-ROM drive.

2. Double-click on the My Computer icon on the Windows desktop (Windows XP users should click on the Start Menu and then click on My Computer). Next, open the Plug-In folder for

whichever application to which you want to install Computones. If you have installed these folders to their default locations, they will be located as follows. The actual plug-in folder names may vary according to software package and version.

Adobe Photoshop 5.0/5.5/6.0/7.0/CS:
  C:/Program Files/Adobe/Photoshop 5.0/Plug-ins
  C:/Program Files/Adobe/Photoshop 5.5/Plug-ins
  C:/Program Files/Adobe/Photoshop 6.0/Plug-ins
  C:/Program Files/Adobe/Photoshop 7.0/Plug-ins
  C:/Program Files/Adobe/Photoshop CS/Plug-ins

Adobe Photoshop Elements 1.0/2.0:
  C:/Program Files/Adobe/Photoshop Elements/Plug-ins
  C:/Program Files/Adobe/Photoshop Elements 2.0/Plug-ins

Jasc Paint Shop Pro 7/8:
  C:/Program Files/Jasc Software Inc/ Paint Shop Pro 7/Plugins
  C:/Program Files/Jasc Software Inc/ Paint Shop Pro 8/Plugins

If you have changed the default installation directories for these applications, then the Plug-In folders will not be located as above.

3. Open up the Plug-Ins folder, create a new folder in it, and rename it "Computones." Open that folder, and create two new folders inside it. Rename one "Computones" and the other "ToneFolder."

4. Open the PlugIn folder on the Computones CD-ROM, select the screentone.8bf file, and drop it into the Computones folder on the local disk.

5. Select the Computones folder on the Computones CD-ROM, and drop it into the ToneFolder folder. The tone file installation is now complete. Next, after starting Photoshop or whichever application you are using, start up Computones → Tones or Multi Tones, click on the Menu button, select Import Tone Set File → View File..., and import the tone file sets you just installed. If you copied tone set files that you do not need, use one of the methods below to remove them.

❶ If there are tones at certain resolutions you do not need, then put the entire 300 dpi or 600 dpi folders in the Recycle Bin to remove them.

❷ If there are certain tone genres you do not need, then open each resolution folder and place the Dot, Hatching, etc. folders in the Recycle Bin to remove them.

Question & Answer

Q I tried running the uninstaller, but I cannot remove Computones!

A If you used a drag-and-drop or copy-and-paste method to install Computones from the CD-ROM, then the ComputonesUninstaller.exe (or "Computones Uninstaller") may not work. In that case, follow the steps below.

1. Double-click on the My Computer icon on the Windows desktop (Windows XP users should click on the Start Menu and then click on My Computer). Next, open the Plug-In folder for whichever application from which you want to uninstall Computones. If you have installed these folders to their default locations, they will be located as follows. The actual folder names may vary according to software package and version.

   Adobe Photoshop 5.0/5.5/6.0/7.0/CS:
   C:/Program Files/Adobe/Photoshop 5.0/Plug-ins
   C:/Program Files/Adobe/Photoshop 5.5/Plug-ins
   C:/Program Files/Adobe/Photoshop 6.0/Plug-ins
   C:/Program Files/Adobe/Photoshop 7.0/Plug-ins
   C:/Program Files/Adobe/Photoshop CS/Plug-ins

   Adobe Photoshop Elements 1.0/2.0:
   C:/Program Files/Adobe/Photoshop Elements/Plug-ins
   C:/Program Files/Adobe/Photoshop Elements 2.0/Plug-ins

   Jasc Paint Shop Pro 7/8:
   C:/Program Files/Jasc Software Inc/ Paint Shop Pro 7/Plugins
   C:/Program Files/Jasc Software Inc/ Paint Shop Pro 8/Plugins

   If you have changed the default installation directories for these applications, then the Plug-In folders will not be located as above.

2. Select the Computones folder in your application's Plug-In folder and drag-and-drop it into the Recycle Bin, or right click on the folder and select Delete from the pop up menu. To completely remove the Computones folder, open the Recycle Bin, and select Empty Recycle Bin from the File menu, or right click on the Recycle Bin and select Empty Recycle Bin from the pop up menu.

Q When I apply a duotone to my image, it looks blurry!

A When you apply a duotone to an image and then display it at 66.6%, 33.3%, or any other magnification other than 100%, it can appear blurry or appear to be "tone jumping." This is due to Photoshop's image interpolation, and there is no actual blurriness present. If you wish to confirm this via your display, be sure to set your magnification factor to 100%.

Q When I print anything out on an inkjet printer, it looks blurry!

A The way inkjet printers print things, it is not possible to print dot patterns precisely as they appear. Also, it may be that the output resolution of the printer you are using and the resolution of the tones in your image are not compatible. This can cause significant blurring or tone jumping. In order to print clearly on an inkjet printer, you must adequately adjust the resolution settings of both the printer and your image.

Q What should I do to print clearly on an inkjet printer?

A If the resolution of the printer you are using and the resolution of the tones in your image are not compatible, blurring or tone jumping can occur. The way inkjet printers print things, it is not possible to print dot patterns precisely as they appear, but by adjusting the output resolution of your printer and the resolution of your image, you can improve print quality and bring it closer to your original work.

1. Verify the output resolution of your printer in your manual.

2. Open your original image in Photoshop. Create multiple working copies of your work for printing purposes.

3. Select Image → Image Size and an Image Size dialog box will appear. Check the Resolution value in the Document Size area. If one of the following conditions applies, proceed to step 4.

   *the inkjet printer resolution = the image resolution
   *the inkjet printer resolution = an even multiple of the image resolution
   *an even multiple of the inkjet printer resolution = the image resolution

If the above conditions do not apply, then your inkjet printer will interpolate the image according to its driver, and the blurriness and tone jumping in your printed image will be worse. In this case, check the Constrain Proportion and Resample Image boxes in the Image Size dialog box, and choose Nearest Neighbor from the Resample Image pull-down menu. Set the Resolution in the Document Size area to match your printer. If your printer's resolution is 1200 dpi or higher, then enter the printer resolution divided by 2 or 4.

4. Click the OK button to apply the current resolution settings, select File → Print..., and print the image. If there is a "Bidirectional Printing" option in your Print dialog, turn it off and then print your image. Leaving this option on may cause tone jumping.

Tone Collection Guide

Dot Tones

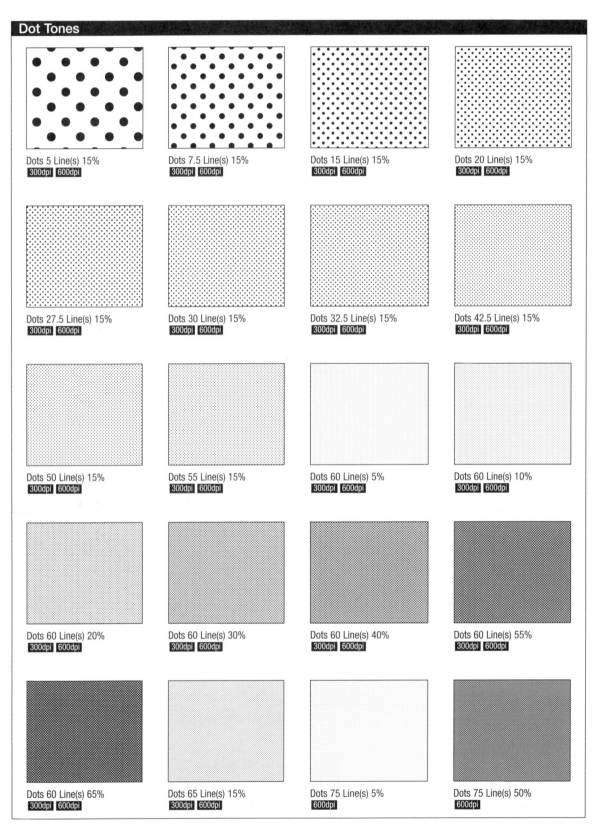

Dots 5 Line(s) 15%
`300dpi` `600dpi`

Dots 7.5 Line(s) 15%
`300dpi` `600dpi`

Dots 15 Line(s) 15%
`300dpi` `600dpi`

Dots 20 Line(s) 15%
`300dpi` `600dpi`

Dots 27.5 Line(s) 15%
`300dpi` `600dpi`

Dots 30 Line(s) 15%
`300dpi` `600dpi`

Dots 32.5 Line(s) 15%
`300dpi` `600dpi`

Dots 42.5 Line(s) 15%
`300dpi` `600dpi`

Dots 50 Line(s) 15%
`300dpi` `600dpi`

Dots 55 Line(s) 15%
`300dpi` `600dpi`

Dots 60 Line(s) 5%
`300dpi` `600dpi`

Dots 60 Line(s) 10%
`300dpi` `600dpi`

Dots 60 Line(s) 20%
`300dpi` `600dpi`

Dots 60 Line(s) 30%
`300dpi` `600dpi`

Dots 60 Line(s) 40%
`300dpi` `600dpi`

Dots 60 Line(s) 55%
`300dpi` `600dpi`

Dots 60 Line(s) 65%
`300dpi` `600dpi`

Dots 65 Line(s) 15%
`300dpi` `600dpi`

Dots 75 Line(s) 5%
`600dpi`

Dots 75 Line(s) 50%
`600dpi`

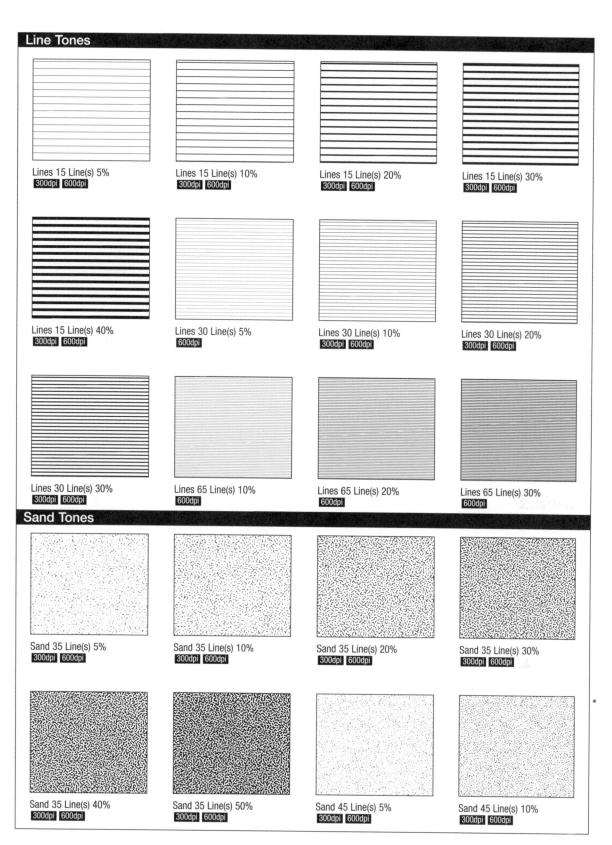

Line Tones

Lines 15 Line(s) 5%
300dpi 600dpi

Lines 15 Line(s) 10%
300dpi 600dpi

Lines 15 Line(s) 20%
300dpi 600dpi

Lines 15 Line(s) 30%
300dpi 600dpi

Lines 15 Line(s) 40%
300dpi 600dpi

Lines 30 Line(s) 5%
600dpi

Lines 30 Line(s) 10%
300dpi 600dpi

Lines 30 Line(s) 20%
300dpi 600dpi

Lines 30 Line(s) 30%
300dpi 600dpi

Lines 65 Line(s) 10%
600dpi

Lines 65 Line(s) 20%
600dpi

Lines 65 Line(s) 30%
600dpi

Sand Tones

Sand 35 Line(s) 5%
300dpi 600dpi

Sand 35 Line(s) 10%
300dpi 600dpi

Sand 35 Line(s) 20%
300dpi 600dpi

Sand 35 Line(s) 30%
300dpi 600dpi

Sand 35 Line(s) 40%
300dpi 600dpi

Sand 35 Line(s) 50%
300dpi 600dpi

Sand 45 Line(s) 5%
300dpi 600dpi

Sand 45 Line(s) 10%
300dpi 600dpi

Tone Collection Guide

Sand Tones

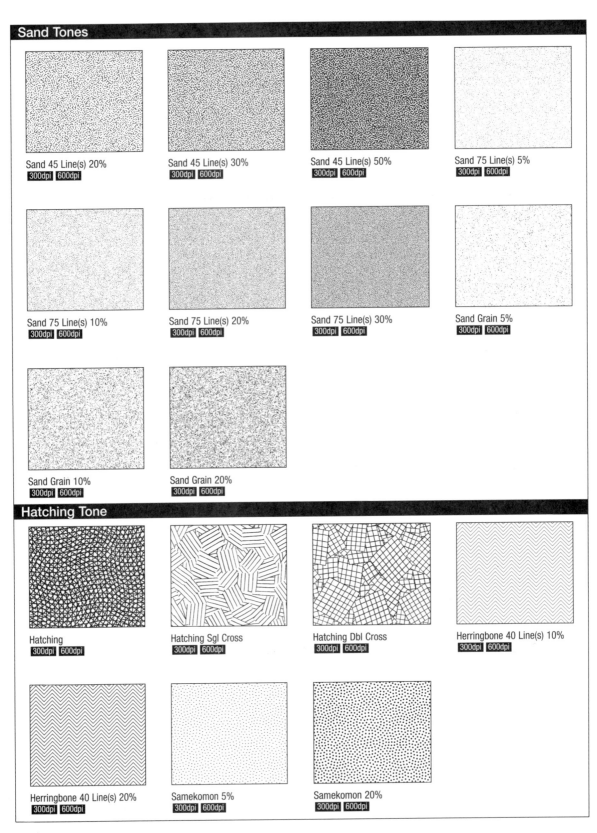

Sand 45 Line(s) 20%
`300dpi` `600dpi`

Sand 45 Line(s) 30%
`300dpi` `600dpi`

Sand 45 Line(s) 50%
`300dpi` `600dpi`

Sand 75 Line(s) 5%
`300dpi` `600dpi`

Sand 75 Line(s) 10%
`300dpi` `600dpi`

Sand 75 Line(s) 20%
`300dpi` `600dpi`

Sand 75 Line(s) 30%
`300dpi` `600dpi`

Sand Grain 5%
`300dpi` `600dpi`

Sand Grain 10%
`300dpi` `600dpi`

Sand Grain 20%
`300dpi` `600dpi`

Hatching Tone

Hatching
`300dpi` `600dpi`

Hatching Sgl Cross
`300dpi` `600dpi`

Hatching Dbl Cross
`300dpi` `600dpi`

Herringbone 40 Line(s) 10%
`300dpi` `600dpi`

Herringbone 40 Line(s) 20%
`300dpi` `600dpi`

Samekomon 5%
`300dpi` `600dpi`

Samekomon 20%
`300dpi` `600dpi`

Gradation Tones

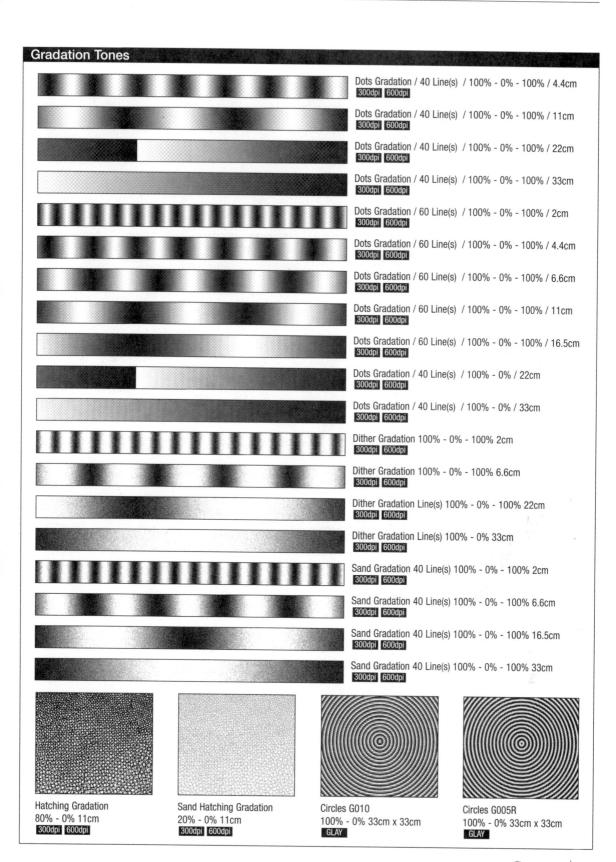

Dots Gradation / 40 Line(s) / 100% - 0% - 100% / 4.4cm
`300dpi` `600dpi`

Dots Gradation / 40 Line(s) / 100% - 0% - 100% / 11cm
`300dpi` `600dpi`

Dots Gradation / 40 Line(s) / 100% - 0% - 100% / 22cm
`300dpi` `600dpi`

Dots Gradation / 40 Line(s) / 100% - 0% - 100% / 33cm
`300dpi` `600dpi`

Dots Gradation / 60 Line(s) / 100% - 0% - 100% / 2cm
`300dpi` `600dpi`

Dots Gradation / 60 Line(s) / 100% - 0% - 100% / 4.4cm
`300dpi` `600dpi`

Dots Gradation / 60 Line(s) / 100% - 0% - 100% / 6.6cm
`300dpi` `600dpi`

Dots Gradation / 60 Line(s) / 100% - 0% - 100% / 11cm
`300dpi` `600dpi`

Dots Gradation / 60 Line(s) / 100% - 0% - 100% / 16.5cm
`300dpi` `600dpi`

Dots Gradation / 40 Line(s) / 100% - 0% / 22cm
`300dpi` `600dpi`

Dots Gradation / 40 Line(s) / 100% - 0% / 33cm
`300dpi` `600dpi`

Dither Gradation 100% - 0% - 100% 2cm
`300dpi` `600dpi`

Dither Gradation 100% - 0% - 100% 6.6cm
`300dpi` `600dpi`

Dither Gradation Line(s) 100% - 0% - 100% 22cm
`300dpi` `600dpi`

Dither Gradation Line(s) 100% - 0% 33cm
`300dpi` `600dpi`

Sand Gradation 40 Line(s) 100% - 0% - 100% 2cm
`300dpi` `600dpi`

Sand Gradation 40 Line(s) 100% - 0% - 100% 6.6cm
`300dpi` `600dpi`

Sand Gradation 40 Line(s) 100% - 0% - 100% 16.5cm
`300dpi` `600dpi`

Sand Gradation 40 Line(s) 100% - 0% - 100% 33cm
`300dpi` `600dpi`

Hatching Gradation
80% - 0% 11cm
`300dpi` `600dpi`

Sand Hatching Gradation
20% - 0% 11cm
`300dpi` `600dpi`

Circles G010
100% - 0% 33cm x 33cm
`GLAY`

Circles G005R
100% - 0% 33cm x 33cm
`GLAY`

Tone Collection Guide

Rendering Tones

Rendering L 01
`300dpi` `600dpi`

Rendering L 01B
`300dpi` `600dpi`

Rendering L 03B
`300dpi` `600dpi`

Rendering L 05
`300dpi` `600dpi`

Radiating DL 01
`300dpi` `600dpi`

Speed Lines 03
`300dpi` `600dpi`

Speed Lines 04
`300dpi` `600dpi`

Rendering L 09B-C
`300dpi` `600dpi`

Rendering L 16-C
`300dpi` `600dpi`

Flash Fills 02
`300dpi` `600dpi`

Flash Fills 04
`300dpi` `600dpi`

Patterned Tones

Sheep
`300dpi` `600dpi`

Kitchen
`300dpi` `600dpi`

Rose
`300dpi` `600dpi`

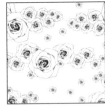

Rose Pattern 02
`300dpi` `600dpi`

Rose Hearts
`300dpi` `600dpi`

Rose Circles
`300dpi` `600dpi`

Sand Hatching WL02
`300dpi` `600dpi`

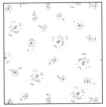

Lace Flowers
`300dpi` `600dpi`

Sand Hatching Fl01
`300dpi` `600dpi`

Sand Hatching Fl02
`300dpi` `600dpi`

Patterned Tones

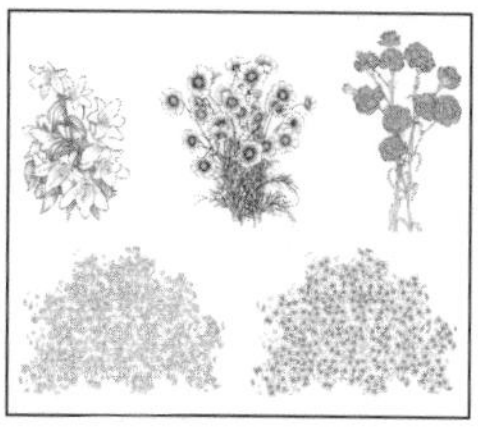

Flowers in Vase
`300dpi` `600dpi`

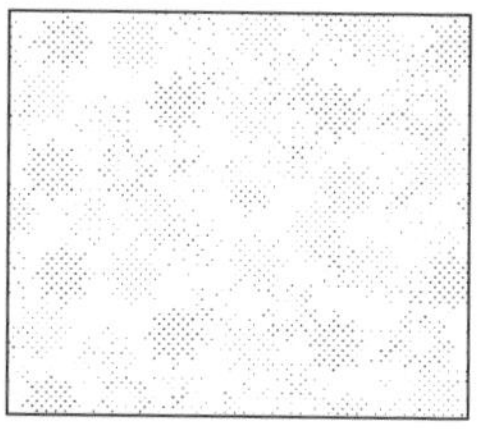

Floral Pattern 04
`GLAY`

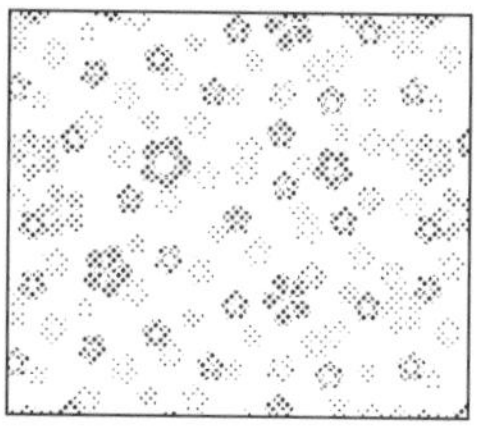

Floral Pattern 02
`GLAY`

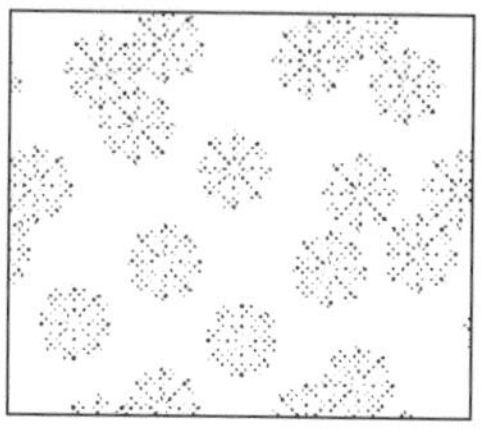

Floral Pattern 03
`GLAY`

School Night K01
`300dpi` `600dpi`

School Noon K01
`300dpi` `600dpi`

Clouds 04
`600dpi` `GLAY`

Clouds 20
`GLAY`

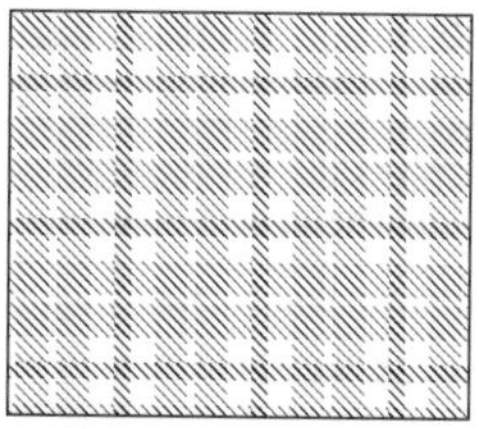

Checker 01
`300dpi` `600dpi`

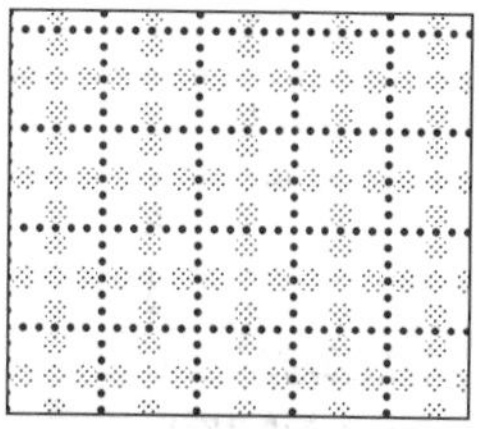

Checker 05
`300dpi` `600dpi`

Checker 07
`300dpi` `600dpi`

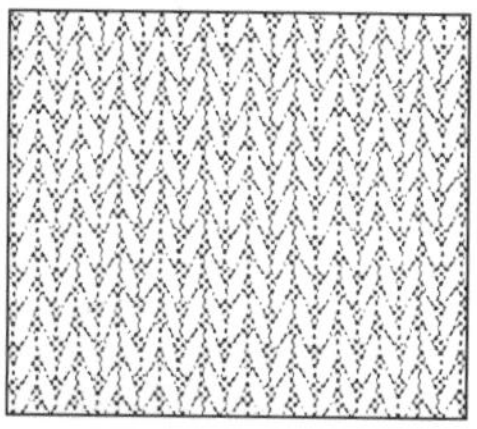

Cotton Weave
`GLAY`

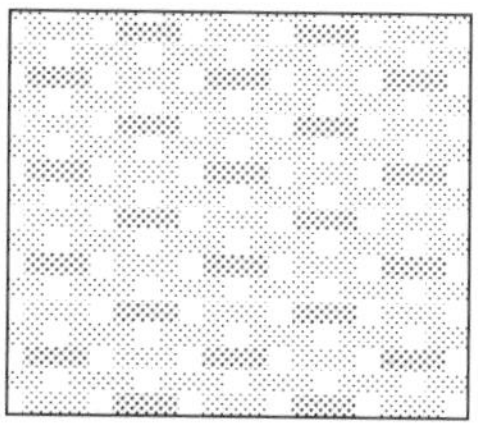

Plain Fablic 02B
`GLAY`

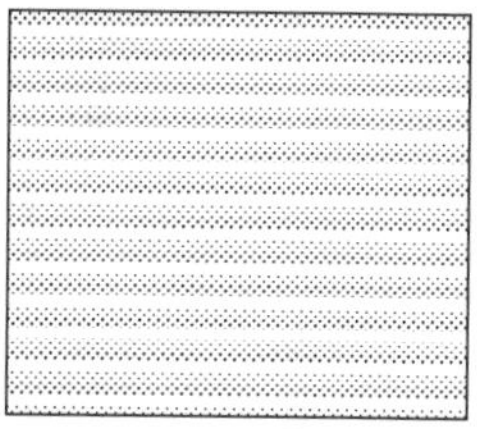

Lines 01
`GLAY`

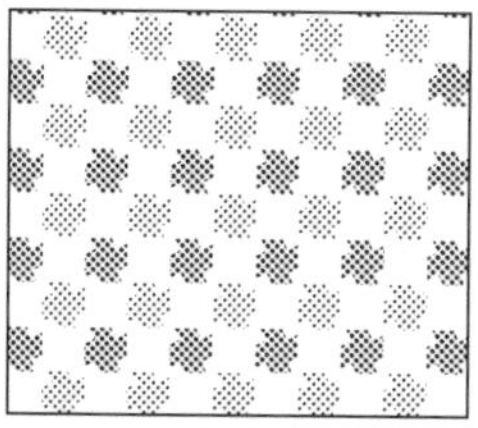

Hounds ToothÅ
`GLAY`

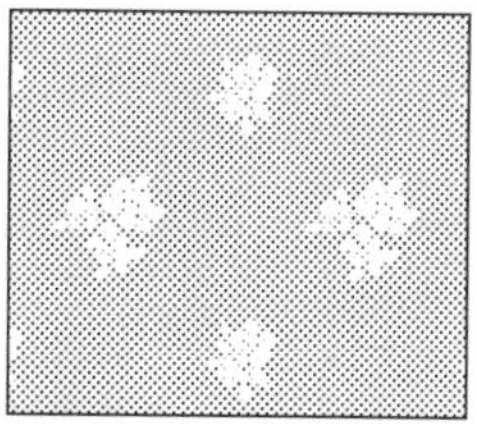

Rose 01
`GLAY`

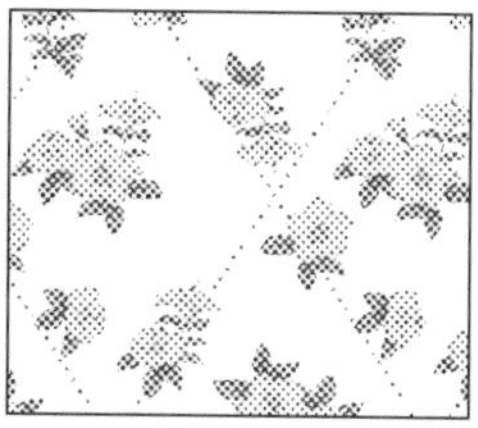

Hibiscus 01
`GLAY`

Tone Collection Guide

Patterned Tones

Train Station 02
`300dpi` `600dpi`

Apt. Buldg. 03_01
`300dpi` `600dpi`

Train Station 03
`300dpi` `600dpi`

Effects Tones

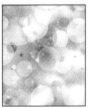
Dots Bubbles 01
`300dpi` `600dpi`

Dots Marble 02
`300dpi` `600dpi`

Sand Hatching H01
`300dpi` `600dpi`

Sand Hatching HS01
`300dpi` `600dpi`

Lightning
`300dpi` `600dpi`

Hatching Lightning
`300dpi` `600dpi`

Sand Hatching LHTG
`300dpi` `600dpi`

Stippled Bubbles F
`300dpi` `600dpi`

Stippled Bubbles
`300dpi` `600dpi`

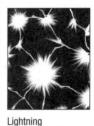

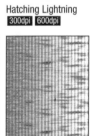

Rain 01
`GLAY`

Rain 02
`GLAY`

Parallel Beams
`GLAY`